W*m*. BEAUMONT's
FORMATIVE YEARS

Two Early Notebooks
1811-1821

William Beaumont
AROUND 1821

Wm. BEAUMONT's
FORMATIVE YEARS

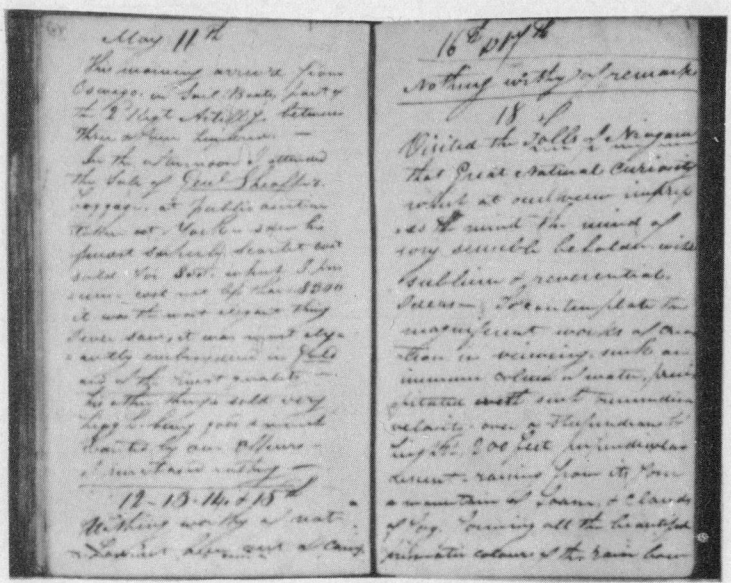

TWO EARLY NOTEBOOKS 1811–1821

With Annotations and an Introductory Essay by

GENEVIEVE MILLER, M.A.

Institute of the History of Medicine
The Johns Hopkins University

Henry Schuman   *New York : 1946*

COPYRIGHT 1946, BY HENRY SCHUMAN, NEW YORK

PRINTED IN THE UNITED STATES OF AMERICA

To

HENRY E. SIGERIST

*pathfinder
in medical history*

CONTENTS

	PAGE
List of Illustrations	vii
Introduction	ix

Part I
    Beaumont's Medical Notebook — 3
        Excerpts from medical authors
        Case histories
        Army medicine
        Prescriptions
    Notes — 34

Part II
    Beaumont's General Notebook — 37
        Literary excerpts
        War and travel diaries
    Notes — 75

Index — 83

LIST OF ILLUSTRATIONS

William Beaumont around 1821	*frontispiece*
	FACING PAGE
Battle of Plattsburg, September 1814	xiv
Jedidiah Morse	xv
A page from Beaumont's notebook	3
Powder-Magazine at Toronto	18
Block-House, Sackett's Harbor	19
The Erie Canal	37
View of Plattsburg	40
The United States Hotel, Plattsburg, N. Y.	41
Sackett's Harbor in 1814	44
Toronto in 1813	45
Map of the Niagara Frontier	48
Queenston in 1812	49
State Prison at Auburn	52
Cayuga Bridge	53
The Port of Buffalo in 1813	54
Put-in-Bay, Lake Erie	55
View of Malden	62
Major General Alexander Macomb	63
Mackinac Island	64
Residence of Isaac C. Platt in Plattsburg, N. Y.	65

[The illustrations are from Benson John Lossing, *The pictorial fieldbook of the War of* 1812, New York, 1868;—John Warner Barber and Henry Howe, *Historical Collections of the State of New York*, New York, 1841;—Cadwallader D. Colden, *Memoir prepared ... at the celebration of the completion of the New York Canals*, New York, 1825. The portrait of Jedidiah Morse was reproduced from James Morse King, *Jedidiah Morse, a champion of New England orthodoxy*, New York, Columbia University Press, 1939, with the kind permission of the publisher.]

INTRODUCTION

ALTHOUGH over one hundred years have passed since William Beaumont made his famous observations on Alexis St. Martin and published the results in his *Experiments and Observations on the Gastric Juice and the Physiology of Digestion* (Plattsburgh, N. Y., 1833), his name still continues in the first rank of American physicians. Without university or even college training, his medical knowledge obtained through association with an older physician, he represents the truly self-educated man, curious and eager to learn. When opportunities for securing additional knowledge presented themselves, whether in personal contacts or in his medical practice, Beaumont possessed the acumen to recognize their value. Even during his first year of practice, when he was an army surgeon in the War of 1812, he demonstrated an honest, critical spirit of inquiry, in observing the progress of patients undergoing various treatments for the same disease, adopting the treatment he found most beneficial, and criticising his fellow surgeons who had unsuccessful results. Hence it was not by accident that he recognized the opportunity which St. Martin's gastric fistula presented, and that he carried his work through, as far as was possible with the existing knowledge of his time.

Without being able to consult university records or curricula to determine the foundations of Beaumont's education, we are extremely fortunate that two of his early notebooks have been preserved* which give us a glimpse into his medical training and early years of practice. They contain fragmen-

* Now in the possession of the Washington University School of Medicine, St. Louis, Mo., where most of the Beaumont documents are preserved. Another important source of manuscript material and relics is the University of Chicago.

Introduction

tary notes from 1811 when Beaumont was still a student, to 1821 when he first went to Ft. Mackinac, at which place the following year the St. Martin episode began. The two books were kept simultaneously, one containing his medical notes and observations, and the other diaries, excerpts from his general reading, and personal reflections of a non-medical character. The diversified pictures which these pages convey: the young student thumbing through Haller's *First Lines of Physiology* in the home of his teacher in a small Vermont town; the surgeon's mate encamped at Sackett's Harbor on Lake Ontario where "the mud and water have been over shoe in every direction, in open huts, without any straw, or more than our blankets to cover us,"* or treating mangled men in the hospital near Niagara after the explosion of the powder magazine at York; the recently appointed post surgeon on his first journey to Ft. Mackinac travelling through the Erie Canal, or in that western wilderness dreaming of his beloved whom he was soon to marry; all these scenes which he himself describes are invaluable to us for an understanding of Beaumont's character and development. The scattered pages of notes from his reading—Shakespeare, Robert Burns, Benjamin Franklin, histories, in addition to his medical books—show his breadth of interest and cultivated taste. When one recalls the unrefinement of backwoods America which was so universally criticised by European travellers of the time, it must have been unusual for a young man to occupy himself on a Lake Erie steamboat by copying verbatim Franklin's "Project for attaining moral perfection," and to spend the winter evenings at Mackinac reading Shakespeare and Anquetil's history.

Born in Lebanon, Connecticut, of old New England stock

---
*Letter to Dr. Benjamin Chandler, April 13, 1813, quoted in Jesse S. Myer, *Life and Letters of Dr. William Beaumont*, St. Louis, C. V. Mosby Co., 1912, p. 36; new print 1939.

Introduction

on November 21, 1785, Beaumont grew up on his father's farm and attended the common school in the village. A restless spirit, he was not content to remain a farmer, so in the winter of 1806-7 he assembled his scanty worldly possessions and started north.* In the spring of 1807 he arrived at Champlain, N. Y., a recently settled village near the lake of the same name and not far from the Canadian border. Here he obtained the position of village schoolmaster. It is not known when his decision to study medicine was made, but while teaching he is said to have used his spare time to read medical books borrowed from a Burlington, Vt., physician. After teaching for three years, he crossed Lake Champlain to St. Albans, Vermont, and entered the home of Dr. Benjamin Chandler as an apprentice in medicine.

Our notebooks begin during the two years that Beaumont lived and studied under Dr. Chandler's roof. While he tells us nothing about his personal life there, we learn that Dr. Chandler was a disciple of the Brunonian system of medicine,† modified somewhat by his own views.‡ Almost immediately Beaumont began to record carefully detailed histories of unusual cases, whether prompted by his teacher or not, we do not know. He had the opportunity to read Haller, Van Swieten, Sydenham, Huxham, Cullen, Brown, Townsend, and Thornton's *Medical Extracts*, all popular textbooks of the day.

Meanwhile the war with England which had been threatening for some time was declared in the summer of 1812. An army was hastily organized and sent to the frontiers of

---

* For biographical details *cf.* Myer, *op. cit.*

† John Brown (1735-1788), a disciple of William Cullen of Edinburgh, who in his book *Elementa medicinae*, 1780, modified Cullen's theory that disease was caused by either increased or diminished activity of the nervous system. Brown stressed, not the nervous energy itself as the cause of disease, but excessive or too feeble stimuli which produced so-called sthenic and asthenic diseases. Because of its clear indications for treatment, it became a very popular system.

‡ *Cf.* Beaumont's letter to Dr. Chandler, Myer, p. 36.

Introduction

Canada. In September, 1812, part of this army was stationed at Plattsburg, N. Y., across the lake from St. Albans. Although Beaumont had already obtained his license to practise medicine the preceding June, he was still living with Dr. Chandler. The presence of the army, which so urgently needed doctors, in his immediate vicinity was a welcome opportunity for the young man to become gainfully employed and useful at once. Not having earned anything for two years, he could only begin private practice burdened with debts. Consequently, even against the wishes of Dr. Chandler, who was politically opposed to the war, Beaumont took his leave and went to the army at Plattsburg where he was immediately appointed surgeon's mate.

During that first winter of the war, the army suffered heavily from the vicissitudes of the northern climate and the lack of proper equipment. Although there were no major engagements, men fell sick and died by the hundreds from intestinal and respiratory disorders. Many of the recruits were unfit for military duty to begin with, many were intemperate, dissolute men who had been unable to make a living as civilians, and who created disciplinary problems as soldiers. The custom of issuing alcohol as part of their rations did not improve the situation. Their poor constitutions, enfeebled by the lack of warm clothing (the government did not provide woolen clothing until this first winter had demonstrated its necessity), fell quick prey to disease, and the crowded unsanitary camps intensified the spread of infection. Little wonder then that James Mann, Hospital Surgeon at this time, reported that out of a group of 5,000 troops, there were seldom more than 3,000 who were fit for duty.*

When spring came, part of the army marched to Lake

---

*James Mann, *Medical Sketches of the Campaigns of* 1812, 13, 14, Dedham, 1816, p. 122.

Introduction

Ontario, where it embarked on an expedition to York (Toronto). Here Beaumont witnessed his first battle, afterwards attending the casualties and retiring with them to a camp near Niagara. While still in that region in the summer of 1813, he stopped writing in his notebooks, and did not continue them during the war. Those notes which we do have, however, depict vividly his everyday experiences and the interest which he took in his patients. Five complete case histories are recorded, together with frequent notes about the treatments which he found most beneficial for the prevailing diseases.

Although we have no personal records of Beaumont's subsequent activities during the war, we know that he continued his duties as a surgeon's mate, and was active at the famous battle of Plattsburg in September, 1814. A letter from Mann, the medical director at Plattsburg at the time, to Surgeon General James Tilton includes him among seven physicians whose conduct during the engagement should be especially commended. Mann wrote, "During the investment of Plattsburgh by the enemy, the surgeons were constantly passing from fort to fort, or block-houses, to dress the wounded, exposed to a cross fire of round and grape shot; while the greater part of the army were covered by fortifications."*

The war being over, Beaumont resigned his commission in order to go into private practice at Plattsburg. This thriving township of over 3,000 inhabitants had been established only 31 years previously by a Revolutionary War veteran from Poughkeepsie, Zephaniah Platt, and his three brothers. Settled mainly by industrious farmers from the New England states, it had developed into a solid community with a newspaper, an academy, a literary club, a medical society, and the county court. Among Beaumont's correspondents mentioned in the one notebook were some of the foremost citizens of the

*Ibid., p. 271.

Introduction

village, and he seems to have developed a reputable practice there. In order to make ends meet in the beginning, he went into partnership with a fellow army surgeon, and the two of them also established a drug and grocery store, a frequent custom among early American physicians. That he never freed himself entirely from financial burdens during this period is shown at the end of one notebook where, before leaving for Mackinac, he listed his creditors. During his residence in Plattsburg he wrote very little in his notebooks.*

Towards the end of 1819, his old restlessness had returned again, and Beaumont gave up his placid village life to become a post surgeon on the frontier. The medical department of the army had been reorganized the preceding year, with his friend and former fellow surgeon Joseph Lovell as Surgeon General. Beaumont applied for reinstatement, and was ordered to Ft. Mackinac in the northwestern wilderness. Now once more he felt the urge to record his daily happenings, and for us today his notes are a fascinating travel log. His remarks as he passed by boat through the recently opened Erie Canal are typical for the wonderment which people felt when modern technology first began to alter the earth's surface.

Among his travelling companions was the Rev. Jedidiah Morse, the venerable clergyman and scholar from Charlestown, Mass., who was the first American geographer and the father of Samuel F. B. Morse. As Morse was somewhat elderly and in poor health, Beaumont attended him throughout the journey to Mackinac and during his stay there. Doubtless the young man derived a great deal of stimulation from this contact, since he wrote in his journal that he anticipated "deriving much benefit and instruction," and later he sent Morse "a specimen of composition."

*At this time he began another notebook, "A Medical & Physical Journal commenced November 1st, 1818, in the sixth year of my medical and surgical practice," also preserved at Washington University, St. Louis.

BATTLE OF PLATTSBURG, SEPTEMBER 1814

(Courtesy of Yale University Art Gallery)

Introduction

Beaumont's notes themselves are more eloquent than any remarks which can be made about them. They are reproduced here, exactly as they stand in the original. Frequent misspellings do not necessarily indicate ignorance, but only haste, since on the following page the same words may stand correctly. The notes from books he was reading are entirely accurate and often copied verbatim. Wherever it has been possible, an attempt has been made to identify personalities and to enlarge the picture of the events which Beaumont mentioned. Large sections of these notebooks have already appeared in print with a few explanatory notes,* but because of their great interest it was felt that a complete edition with detailed notations would be worthwhile.

I wish to express my sincerest thanks to the Washington University College of Medicine, St. Louis, Mo., for the kind permission to publish these notebooks which are in its possession, to Dr. Henry E. Sigerist of the Johns Hopkins University for his advice and criticism, and to Dr. Arno B. Luckhardt of the University of Chicago for his friendly assistance in obtaining illustrations.

GENEVIEVE MILLER.

Institute of the History of Medicine
The Johns Hopkins University

---

* *Cf.* Myer, *op. cit.*, pp. 21-27, 38-55, 74-85.

Wm. BEAUMONT's *FORMATIVE YEARS*

Two Early Notebooks
1811-1821

PART I

Near the middle of November the Army march'd from Plattsburg to the Province Line, 45 D.y. rout taking no tents & destitute of of covering, save a Blanket or two, lying out in open air, after, marching all day through the mud & water, & thus expos'd to the inclemencies of the weather for a week encamp't in the woods, after which, the army return'd to Plattsburgh & there encamp'd again in the woods without Tents or Huts, the first night which was very rainy & cold, the second also was wet & windy. They then mov'd to Swanuts & encamp'd again in the woods, during which time

A PAGE FROM BEAUMONT'S NOTEBOOK

PART I
Beaumont's Medical Notebook

Excerpts from medical authors.
Case histories. Army medicine.
Prescriptions.

HALLER. Attention is when one Idea occupies the mind principaly or solely for any length of time—

The comparison of any two Ideas instituted by the mind, is called judgement.

Genius consists in a vivid sensation conjoined with rapidity of thought, so as instantly to abstract from notions their points of similitude or dissimilitude

The principal source of judgment, invention & wisdom, consists in the slow examination of Ideas, by which they are considered by the mind in every point of view and in the attention of the mind being confined to one object, to the exclusion of all other Ideas——Hallar—[1]

13ⁿ Finery is the affectation of dress and very often covers a great deal of dirt

INTERMITANTS——

Causes—Marsh Miasmata—damp houses, evening dews, lying on the ground, or whatever relaxes the solids, diminishes perspiration or obstructs the circulation, disposes the body to agues——

Symtoms—Pain in the head, loins, weariness of the limbs, coldness of the extremities, with sometimes great sickness of the Stomach—

Regimen. Acidulated drinks, mucilages, Broths, wine whey &c. with sometimes, twenty or thirty drops of Laudanum in a dose soon after the commencement of a hot fit—

Beaumont's Medical Notebook

But the principal intentions of cure are to brun the solids & promote perspiration——

M.M.[2] Evacuations, by Emetics & cathartics, in the first instance, bleeding to be omitted, unless an inflamatory diathesis indicate its use—such as excessive heat & delirium—

Thin the bark, plentifully or sparingly as the case may be—

ACUTE FEVERS—

Cause Arise from causes similar to those of Intermittansts—

Symtoms—A chillness or rigour in the beginning of the fit, succeeded by great heat, frequent & full puls., pain of the head, dry skin, redness of the eyes, florid countenance, difficulty of breathing, sickness with an inclination to vomit, great thirst —no appetite, black & rough tonge, delirium, laboruous respiration.

These symtoms indicating to great heat a rigidity of the vessels & consequently an obstruction of all the secretions—require diluting drinks such as barley-water, balm-tea, & apple juice, Panada[3] &c &c——

M.M. Bleeding first, indicated in case of a hard, full, quick pulse, as soon as the inflamatory symtoms appear—& should be repeated untill they are diminished—If the heat & fever be very great, *Niter* &c &c &c &c

But if the patients spirits grow languid, his pulse sink, breathing becomes difficult, with stupor, trembling of the nerves, with twitching of the tendons—there is danger. In this case Epistpastics to the head ancles & thighs &c—drafts to the soles of the feet, cordials, wine &c——

SPOTTED FEVER—

Causes Foul air, arising from putrid animal or vegetable substances,—living too much on animal substances, or eating fish or flesh that is become putrid, or inclining to it——

Beaumont's Medical Notebook

Symtoms. Great debility without any apparent cause, violent pain in the head, laborious breathing, pain about the region of the Stomach, back & lions, tremors & delirium—Blood drawn appears disolved in with a very small degree of cohesion & soon becomes putrid—stools feotid, sometimes of a greenish, black or redish cast,—spots upon the skin, small pulse great dejection of mind. This fever may be distinguished by the foregoing symtoms as being more violent than the nervous—

M.M. An emetic, in the first attack may be given with probable advantage, but after three or four days if the symtoms be violent are to be omitted as hurtful. The body must be kept open by gentle clysters or mild cathartics— Bleeding seldom to be used unless there be signs of inflamation, or sometimes in the first onset, but the repitition generally is hurtful. Blisters, are never to be used unless in the greatest extremeties, such as the sudden disapearance of petechiæ, a remarkable sinking of the pulse & a delirium.

Wine with acids & antiseptics are the only things to be relied on in the cure of malignant fevers—The Bark, when the purple livid & black spots appear, must [be] administered in large doses & long presisted in—

Formula Tincture of the Bark, acidulated with spirits of Vitriol, when the Petechiae appear.

Pleurisy. Is an inflamation of the Pleura—Occasioned by whatever obstructs the perspiration—

Symtoms—generally begins with chilliness & shivering, succeeded by heat, thirst, & restlessness.—The pulse in this disease is commonly quick & hard, if blood be let, it is covered with a tough crust or buffy coat—the urine high colour'd,—the Spittle first thin, afterwards thick, & sometimes streaked with blood———

Regimen. as in other febrile and inflamatory cases

M.M. Venesection, repeated if necessary, till the stitch in the side abate & the violence of the symtoms subside, fomentations, Epispastics to the part most affected—expectoration assisted by oily & mucilaginous drinks, oxymels as Vinegar of Squills &c———

Miss Maria Allen, was taken on the 12th of August, 1811, with the common autumnal fever,—the symtoms very favorable, & its progress mild without the least aprehension of danger, till the eighth day (being excessively hot, & swealtering), just at night, when she was discovered by her Physicians, to have fallen into a state of extreme debility & fast sinking, as if under a powerful internal Hemorrhagy, & notwithstanding every medicine that was administred for her relief, not a momentary effect could be procur'd, but she continued to fail faster & faster for about two hours, when, to the heart-felt grief & inexpressible sorrow of her tender mother & affectionate brothers,—she expired, amidst the groans & lamentations of her sympathetic companions, & congenial friends & associates delluged in tears of grief, for the loss, so amiable a *daughter*, *Sister*, friend & companion——

The body was immediately open'd, where was found, in a fluid form the *Omentum*, almost completely disolv'd only about two or three ounces, remaining, that in any respect, retaind the form or texture of a *Caul*—a quart or more of Ol. found in the cavity of the Abdomen, & a quantity of blood in the first passage, probably an *Hemorrhagy* from the *Hemorrhoidal* vessels & (detached from the cause or effect of the present disease) the *Ovaria*, enlarged to more than three times their natural size, filled both externally & internally with Hydatids, & many of them in a state of actual supuration, which last circumstance would unavoidably have circumscrib'd the number of her days to a very contracted period——

From Saunder's[4] experiments, it seems that the constituent parts of the *Bile* are first *water*, which contains the odor. 2^d. a *mucilage* of an albuminous nature. 3^d. a *resin*, containing the colour & taste, & a mineral alkali, which last is the basis———

The Biliary concretions, seem compos'd of calcarious earth, with the mineral & volatile alkali, as common salt & Sal. Ammon.———

Beaumont's Medical Notebook

Formula of Pill for urinary or any other calculus concretions Sal Soda or Natron form'd with soap into pill.

The mind that can amuse itself with the *love-sick trash*, of most modern compositions of *novel reading*; seeks enjoyment beneath the level of a rational being—

Mr. Reynolds, a strong, robust & vigorous, constitution was committed to Goal, for "lying with another man's wife" under the debilitating influence of the *State's Prison*

He was put into [a] cold underground room, in the month of Novr. without any fire, additional apparrel, or bedding with open grates, & a free circulation of air—wet, cold or dry

He remain'd in this situation for four or five weeks, when he was taken ill with Symtoms & &c &c &c &c &c &c—& run away & liv'd or died I cant tell which—

April 22^d 1812—Mary-Maria, Daughter of J—— W— had been for many months, very much out of health, feeble & complaining, of much pain & distress, she not being old enough to tell the nature or exact seat of her complaint, her Parents, suppos'd her to be troubled with Worms, & accordingly, gave her vermifuge medicine, without the desired effect, she still continued ailing, & from the history of her Parents she appear'd singular at times by seeming to be troubled with the presence of some hateful undesirable object, at which she would strike, & contend with, th° nothing was there—quarrelling with the children—seeming patulent, & feverish, & complaining of her head, more particularly.—On, or about, the 12th of Instant she was violently attacked with a Pulmonic Inflamation which continued obstinate, with a pale sunken countenance, cold extremeties, with occasional flushings of fever & burning heat, freequent stopage of circulation, nausea, vomiting, & universal dryness of skin, until about the 10th day of the disease, when she was taken, (as the people suppos'd) with a fit, that is an affection of the nerves, a twitching of the mussles, a wild staring delirium, dilatation of the pupils, continual picking with the fingers, at nothing, making a kind of whimpering noise & crying, complaining of great heat & pain in the head,

& a continued nausea & sickness. Tho there were but a forlorn hope of recovery, it was propos'd & she put into the cold bath, which seem'd to give short relief from the violent symtoms but they soon returned, & notwithstanding a repitition of the bath, to no effect she died in about 8 hours after the first imersion at 2 oclock, A.M.—The symtoms of the hydrocephalus Internus, having been so obvious, it was conceived to be productive of future benefit, to open the head—leave being obtain'd, it was accordingly done on the same day, at about one oclock P.M. where we found about half a pint of serous fluid, contain'd in the ventricles & diffus'd thro the substance of the brain, the blood vessels all distended with thick black blood, the whole substance of the brain of a cinericious a rather watery appearance & the dura mater firmly adhering to the skull all around as well as at the sutures & bore evident marks of an inflamation of the membranes of the brain

---

A.M. A healthy young Lady of full plethoric habit of body, (though not of a very strong constitution,) was, on the 17th of August, seized with a Synocha or inflamatory fever. Symtoms violent, & weather extremely warm & sultry—for several days previous to this attack, she had been quite unwell, but keept about her usual domestic employment, taking heavy doses of Laud. to relieve pain till about 10, oclk. on the 17th she was taken with violent pains in her head, Side, back, loins, muscles & limbs, cold chills, rigors, universal lassitude, and nausia—face red as scarlet, eyes inflamed, & great soreness on motion—tongue thick coated & very black, skin dry & hot, & puls. strong, full & hard.

I was call'd about 11.OC.—immediately took about 14 ℥ blood—gave an emetic, cum Pill cathartic, which evacuated much foul black billious matter from the stomach, & from the bowels, besides a spontaneous bleeding from the orifice in the Arm of about 12 ℥ as near as could be judg'd, which reduced the high arterial action & much abated the other violent symtoms, & with the assistance of the Saline draught induced a free perspiration, & pretty much relieved her pains—continued the Saline Draught, with the addition of the Dover's Powders,[5] thr° the night which afforded a pretty comfortable night's rest, & kept up a general action in the system, tho there was some prostration of strenght, & slight pains & dizziness of the head—Thr° the fore part of [the] following day —with a slight paroxism of fever about eleven—In the after part of the day, the pain in her head increased with the recurrence of some of the other symtoms, & I judged further evacuations from the bowels to be necessary, & accordingly promoted it by *cal. & Ol Ricin* which after a pretty severe operation, left her considerably exhausted, notwithstanding a free use of the Pulvs. Dovr. & Serpt. Virg[6]—The next morning, after a night of considerable pain & distress, in consequence of the continuation of the Alterant Pills[7] kept up during the operation of the Physic, th° reliev'd in the morning by an opiate—She continued better thr° the day—took Ol Ricini at night which after operating, left her in the same condition as before, griping in consequence of the *Pill. Alterans.* & reliev'd in the same way, tho much affected with dyspnoea & faintness—Saturday morning—Bark, Wine, Serpturia, & Brunan. Pill.[8] continued to be administered with a liberal hand—broth & friction given freely, yet notwithstanding all these she continued to have faint turns, with cold extremeties with considerable sinking of the pulse thro' the day, which may be ascribed, partly, perhaps, to the shock given her by the bell's tolling for the death of a child in the neighbourhood —at night directed the stimuli to be increased—added Calombo to the Serpt—rested very well thro the night,— much better this morning—Strenght sufficient to rais herself up—Sets up considerable, quite free from pain,—takes nourishment with a good relish, action much better,—capilaries free—passages regular,—some troubled with dyspnœa,—but on the whole must be considered on the convalescence state— Sunday afternoon—Monday week, so far recovered as to ride in Waggon to Cambridge, 20 miles in a a day, got married, & enjoyed—good health, &c &c—

Beaumont's Medical Notebook

September 13th 1812—
> Commenced practice in the U. S.'s Army, as Surg's Mate of the 6th Reg^t Infy—
> *Prevailing type of Disease,*—[9]
> *Intermittents, Typhus, Dysentaries, & Rheumatism*—
> *Treatment*, of Intermittent—in the first instance, gave an Emetic of Tart. Ant. followed with a brisk cathartic of Jalap, Rhei. Ol Ricin. Sometimes combin'd with *Cal.*—then Sudorifics chiefly Antimonials, & Alkalies—& a free use of the bark in *Decoc.*—which treatment generally effected a recovery in a week or ten days,—tho some obstinate cases, run on for three or four weeks, terminating in Typhus Gravior in which, I gave bark wine, Opium, Serpentaria, & the Brunonian Pill, with a liberal hand & with very good success, not loosing more than one out of fifty.—But from a particular learnt, that, small & often repeated doses of Ipecac, Emet Tart & Opii. with the Saline Draught were preferable to any other mode of practice —The Ipecac or Emt Tart. in doses from ½ to grain evry three hours, with half grain Opii, had an astonishing effect in cleansing the prima viae—cleaning the tongue of the foul dark coat, & opening the cutaneous pores, & of course aleviating the symtoms—Cal in extreme low cases, was had recourse to with wonderful success, in doses from ss gr. to gr.—evry three hours till the Glands were touched, especially when there was an affection of Lungs which was generally the case in the Hospital at this time—The Bark & wine were in most cases of Typhus detrimental & often fatal as was obvious from that fatal practice in some of the other departments of the Army. Instance 15th Reg—who died at the rate of two out of three under that practice——

> In Dysintaries,—& Diorrhoes half a grain of Opii. with half a grain Ipecac, & a simple solution of Sal Natron were generally sufficient to carry off the disease,——

> The Rheumatism, in the exposed situation in which the men were placed, was very difficult to cure, the Opium, Guaiac, &

Spirits Terebinth were most useful, in checking the pain, sometimes removing them, but not often—

Near the Middle of November the Army mov'd from Plattsburg to the Province-Line, 45 Deg. north[10] taking no tents & destitute of covering, save a Blanket or two, lying out in open air, after marching all day through the mud & water, & thus expos'd to the inclemencies of the weather for a week encampt in the woods, after which, the army return'd to Plattsburgh & then encamp'd again in the woods without Tents or Huts, the first night of which was very rainy & cold, the Second also was wet & windy. They then mov'd to Saranac, & encamp'd again in the woods,—during which time the weather was very various warm & cold sometimes raining, sometimes snowing, the men lying upon the cold wet ground, with only a fire before their tents, for two, three or four weeks.—[11]

Whilst in this wretched & deplorable situation the men were seized with *Dysentary*, Intermittants, Pleurisy, Peripneumony, Cynanchy, & Rheumatism, which made the very woods ring with coughing & groanings———

The Dysentary, I found soon yielded to the use of the Opium & Ipecac, in doses of half a grain each, or to a grain of Opium at night & half a grain in the morning without the Ipecac—some however would run on, & terminate in Typhus.

Intermittants were found to yield to the use of Opium & Tart. Ant. in doses of half a grain of the former combin'd with a grain of the latter evry three or four hours—when the Stomach was foul it first requir'd a full Emetic of Tart. Emt. & the Intestines cleard by brisk cath^c.—

In Pleurisy & Peripneumony bleeding on the first attack, till the symtoms subsided, was the most salutary of any thing & when omitted was always regretted—as it very much retarded the recovery of the patient, & increased the violence of disease—After one copious bleeding the use of Opium, Glyc. Senn Tart. Ant. & Digitalis in equal proportions by bulk were verily efficatious in relieving the Cough, & generally the only medium required to cure the disease. Blistering became necessary in obstinate cases when bleeding did not relieve the

Beaumont's Medical Notebook

Stitch, in the side & pain in the head which it seldom ever fail'd of doing—when had recourse to in time—

This treatment of the foregoing diseases I am warranted in adapting—from the happy issue & successful termination of more than two hundred cases out of which not one has died while under my care.—

Some cases ran on for some time, terminating in a bilious remittant, with a continual vomiting, & rejecting evry thing taken in the stomach,—with Diarrhea in which cases, the mucilage of Gum Arabic, & Elix. Vit. have soon corrected the iritability of the stomach, & saved the patient which otherwise must have died.—

Tuesday, December 8th Weather warmish, & cloudy, air damp, ground thawing, & wet, men complaining of Dysentary, Pleurisy, & Peripneumony,—bleed without measure or weight, give Opium & Ipecac for Dysent^y.— Opium, Glyc. Tart. Ant. & Digit., in pleurisy Peripneumony—& have the happiness to see my patients recovering daily under the treatment—Evening—damp & chilly—men lying in tents, with small fires in front——

Wednesday Decr. 9th, 1812—

Weather chilly, & cloudy several new cases, this morning the old ones doing well under the former treatment—cough subsiding, pains diminishing & apetite amending,—gave, this morning, the *Anti Dysenteric* Pill,[12] to those who were complaining of bad relax—In the Typhoid cases, gave Opium, Ipecac, Tart. Ant. half a grain each evry three hours with evident good effects—In the case of one, Covet, who has been for two weeks very low with the Typhus so as to be unable to help himself or even to take scarce any nourishment on his stomach without immediately rejecting it followed with a constant straining to vomit—he was seized last night with a most excrutiating pain in his left side extending from his hip to the top of his left shoulder, so severe was the pain that he could scarce breath without screaming his extremities cold, & no pulsation to be felt—Indeed I thought he would have died in spite of medicine but by giving 60 gtts. Laud. Liq. repeated in about fifteen minutes with the use of warm fomentations, he got easier, arterial action was restor'd, & he made quite comfortable thrº the night by repeating the Laud^m evry two hours, in doses of 15 gtts. at a time—The Elix. Vitriol in doses of 12 gtts evry two hours with a tablespoonful of the mucilage of Gum Arabic was the first thing that would check the vomiting & nausea, to day his stomach bears food in small quantities—no vomiting this day—but very weak.—Wednesday evening 8^{oc}.

Thursday Morning 11^{oc}.
Men in Hospital better—Covet continues to mend under the use of Laud^m Elix Vit. & Broth—Several new cases, of Pleurisy, Peripneumony & Dysenty in which I continue to bleed, give opium, Tart Ant. & Ipecac with evident success, many that came yesterday being able to do duty to day—

Friday 11^{oc}. Weather cold, & falling snow,—not but few new cases, this morning,—all in Hosp^{l}. much better,—Covet continues to mend under the former treatment,—giving to day, a Deco^{c} of Guaiac & Serpt Virg.—Typhus yields to the use of Ipecac & opii, & nourishment———

Saturday morning 11^{oc}. 12 day
Men in Hospital doing well, most of them convallescent—continue the same treatment—There are four new cases—principally Intermittents, one Pneumonia—*Covert* [Covet?], mending fast,—Dysentary, & Diarrhea yields to the use of the Anti Dysenteric Pill in two & three days—

Saturday Evening. 9^{oc}.

Remarks Ascertaind the treatment of the Surgeon (Gilluland)[13] of the 16th Reg. in this camp disease, now prevailing, which is to give from one to three Emts. & as many cathartics, in order, he says, to cleans the Prima viæ, & aleviate the symtoms of a bilious diarrhea, & then give tonics—Behold the *gasping* gasping Mortals how they die!—from, two to five in a day!—twenty six in the course of two weeks out of four hundred,—Can it be correct practice, when, in the next Reg.—out of Six hundred in an exactly similar situations & labouring under the same diseases not one has died in the same time under a

Beaumont's Medical Notebook

diametrically opposite practice?—No!! depletion by bloodletting & antimonial sudorifics & diaphoretics, & an entire disuse of all tonic medicines is the proper plan of cure.

Suspended Duty in the Army from the 1st
1st January 1813, till the 15th February——[14]

Commenced Boarding with Doct Bradford,[15] 19th Feb^y

Peripneumonics, prevailing in Camp,—Serg^t Fulton taken violently with all the alarming symtoms,—was bleed in the first instance, & Blisterd, which reliev'd the pain in the side partially,—yet he was labouring under dispnoea, with pain & stricture across his breast—dry skin, general lassitude & a great watchfulness, some times delirious, & very weak—gave the alterant Pill,—barley tea Antimonials, Elix. Paregoric & applied another blister, which treatment very much releivd Symtoms, by promoting a free expectoration, & gentle diaphorisis. On the 4th day—gave the wine moderately, with the mucilage of barley,—a decoction of the Seneka & Serp^t Virg. under which treatment he continues to mend th^o very moderately on account of the negligence of his attendance—March 1st—Recov^d————

Taken on the 17th Feby. 1813, Lewey, De Frenchman, with the common, but more violent, symtoms of Peripneumony,—was bled by Doct B——^{d}, but perhaps to no great advantage it seeming to increase the pains—I found him extremely debilitated, in excessive pain, great difficulty of breathing, stricture across the breast, tongue, dark dry & husky, perspiration entirely suppres'd with delirium—Order'd bathing with warm hemlock Tin,[16] extensively, humid baths to his feet,—gave the alterant powders of opii, Ipecac, & cal. evry two hours,—applied blisters to the breast—gave the Elix Pareg^c with Tart. Ant.—with two drops Ol Cin, & twelve of Ether Vit. evry 4 hours,—for nourishment, gave the barley tea—with wine—In 36 hours, he began to mend & continues so to do under the use of wine, barley water, & Brunonian Pill—this being the

[14]

Beaumont's Medical Notebook

14th day of the disease, he free from pain, breathing free, & free capilaries,—his tongue clear, & appetite fast amending—indeed he is conval^t

Recov^d————

James McMullen, having long laboured under Tisis Pulm. died on the 25th Feby with an Hemorragy from the Lungs, in consequence of a violent fit of coughing——

Sundry cases of Peripneumony all yielding to the foregoing treatment of this disease—

The Sixth Reg^t march^d from Plattsburgh, on the 19th of March, 1813,[17]—The weather, cold 1st day, warm & pashy—some of the men marching over shoe in snow & water, the rest riding in Sleys,—1st night, lay out in open air,—the next day, cold & rainy—men riding, kept out till 12 oc^k P.M. & then to lie in barns, or in open air,—but few complaining, none left behind in consequence of sickness—3^d day clear & cold—4th snow'd in the morn'^{g}—clear & pleasant in the latter part,—at night men in good quarters—5th pleasant and thawing—6th also pleasant—7th cold, 8th clear, thawing, but chilly south wind, arrivd at Sackett Harbour leaving not a sick man behind—encampt at night in open huts,—9th day, a few complaining of Intermittant types—10th one or two cases of Pneumonic symtoms—none confin'd—11th, some, complaining of Intermittants not one confind—to bed or bunk[18]

April 1st 1813. Sacketts harbour[19]

Type of disease. *Intermittants* in many cases complicated with Pneumony.—Symtoms in general—universal pain in the bones & mussles, cold chills, nausea & pain in the head and breast,— sometimes, accompanied with acute local pain in the side, with cough, & other evident Pneumonic symtoms—Treatment—When Pneumonic symtoms most prevail,—use the lancet early in the attack, Epispastics & Antimonials. In the Intermittant Type,—give the *Pillule Chandler*, a Tart Ant. & cal. so as to puke & purge smartly—followed with the Pill Brunon. a Tart Ant. et call[20] in alterant doses—to dry—

Beaumont's Medical Notebook

From Sackett's Harbour, the Troops embarked, on board the fleet, about 1500, in 14 vessels, 1 Ship, 1 Brig & 12 Sch[rs]—3 Companies of our Reg[t] were on board the Sch[r]. *Julia* (Capt Trent com[dg]) we were 5 days from the harbour, to York[21], tho our men were very much crowded both in the hole & on Deck, we had none remaining on board when we debarked, all were able to fight like good fellows—4 or 5 were left sick on board the other vessels of our Reg[t]—not any of ours were wounded in the engagement—but by the explosion of the Magazine, our Reg[t] suffer'd more than any other, being the most advanced body, & within ¼ mile of explosion—a most shocking scene ensued, the stones falling thick as hail in all directions, cut bruis'd & mangled the men most shockingly, about 60 were killed dead on the spot,—(20 of ours) & 250 wounded, of which 109—belong'd to our Reg[t] their wounds were of the worst kind, comp[d] fractures of *legs, thighs & arms & fractures of Sculls*,—on the night of the explosion, we were all night engaged in amputating & dressing the worst of them—the next day also, & the day after. I perform'd four amputations & 3 trepaning—on the fourth day after we came into the Brittish Garrison we were ordered to get the sick & wounded on board—they were crowed into the vessels indiscriminately, with their respective companies, & remain in this condition for 8 days. Some of the worst of the wound, were not even dressed in the mean time.—in consequence of the Surgeons not being able to attend the several vessels on account of the boisterous wind & storm which prevaild for the whole time.

Besides the wounded there were numerous cases of Dysen[ys] & Diarrheas prevailing—& some cases of Typhus fevers, at least on board the Julia, & I presume more in many of the other vessels.

May 14th Camp near Niagara.

Some cases of Typhus, & a few intermittents, but the principal business at present is to dress wounds rec[d] at the battle of York, or rather in the explosion of the Magazine—all lacerations & contusions—the compound fractures & amputations being sent to the hospital—

NB. James Bartlett, a soldier of the 6th Inf[ty], rec'd a severe contusion, at the time of the explosion, on the Glutii Mussle of the left side,—had nothing done to it for near two week—at this time he came to me with a soft fluctuating tumor, on the point of buttock, surrounded by a hard circular edge, no inflamation, but had some sharp, throbing pains, & soreness—I directed emolient pultices for 24 hours,—it appeared softer but no redness ensued.—I then directed him to continue the pultices 24 hrs longer.—then on close examination there are evident appearance of much fluid matter, either of puss or extravasated blood, but from its livid, dull & indurated appearance conceiv'd it be the latter, & to ascertain I puncturd & found nothing but black grumous blood, which discharg'd not very freely—I then directed a poultice of black alder bark & flower, to be applied constantly (as there was nothing else to be procured in the situation we were then in—

15th this morning the tumor more soft—but no puss appears yet

16 Tumor continues to abate pain less, & continues to discharge grumous blood—to the relief of the pain, no puss—Came to mature superation & recoverd.—

A singular case of Fracture—
cranium on a Soldier, wounded in the attack at Newark with a musket ball, & put in the General Hospital 28th May.—
A singular case of fractured cranium, by a musket ball in the Battle of Newark (UC)[22] 27th May—1813—

A Soldier rec[d] the Ball on the upper & right edge of the Occipital Bone, directly over the latteral sinus. The ball lodged under the integuments, & depressed a piece of the bone about 1½ inch long & ¾ inch broad, running in a direction from the superior part of the os occipitis towards the right ear, it was depressed the whole thickness of the skull,—the patient complaind very little of any pain or uneasiness for 8 or 10 days, —no evident symtoms of depression appear'd—had a good appetite,—could walk about without inconvenience,—complained sometimes of sickness of the Stomach & vertigo—his countenance was rather sallow & wan but not comatose at all

Beaumont's Medical Notebook

—On a thorough examination of the case & due consideration of the probable event of such a wound—the depressed part being entirely dead,—Doct Daniel[23] (Hosp¹ Surg︠n︡ Gnl) Doct Lovell[24] & myself, thought it advisable to trepan without delay, judging from the nature of the case, that the injured bone must exfoliate sooner or later & kill the patiant if not remov'd, therefore the oppration was perform'd by Doct Lovell in a most adroit & masterly manner,—on perforating the sound edge of the bone above the depressed portion, the trephine at one side seem'd quickly thr°, but the other requir'd considerable longer & cautious labour befor it appeard through—no hemorrhagy ensued—till the circular was raised by the levator,—when the blood gushed from the lateral sinus, in a stream as large as my little finger—threatning instant death—but Doct Lovell by compressing the lascerated sinus with his finger, till the fractured pieces could be taken out, & then firmly compressing it with soft lint, perfectly secur'd it from bleeding—put on the dressings, & the patient got up and walked about as before, apparently[25]

Ps 139th [26]
The wonders of *God* in the formation of Man—

---

1   When I with pleasing wonder stand,
    And all my features view,
    Lord 'tis thy work; I own thy hand,
    Thus built my humble clay.—
2   Thy hand my heart & reins possess,
    Where unborn nature grew;
    Thy wisdom all my features trac'd
    And all my members drew.
3   Thine eye with nicest care survey'd
    The growth of ev'ry part,
    Till the whole scheme thy thoughts had laid
    Was copied by thy art.—
4   Heaven, Earth & Sea & fire & wind,
    Show me thy wondrous skill,

POWDER-MAGAZINE AT TORONTO.

BLOCK-HOUSE, SACKETT'S HARBOR.

Beaumont's Medical Notebook

But I review myself & find,
Diviner wonders still.—
5 Thy awful glowries round me shine
My flesh proclaims thy praise,
Lord, to thy works of nature join,
Thy miracles of Grace—

From nature's continent immensely wide,
Immensly small this little Isle of life
This dark incarcerating colony divides us.
————Happy day that break the chain
That manumits; that calls from exile home
That leads to Nature's great metropolis
And readmits us thr° the guardian hand
Of elder brother, to a father's throne.
Who hears our advocate, & thr° his wounds
Beholding man, Allows the tender name.
'Tis this makes Christian triumph great,
'Tis this makes joy a duty to the wise,
'Tis impious in a good man to be sad—
Young[27]
Sylvius.De.la.Boe[28]

Earth, on whose lap a thousand nations tread
And Ocean brooding his prolific head,
Night's changful orb, blue pale & silv'ry runs
Where other worlds enrich other suns,
One mind inhabits, one diffusive soul,
Wields the large limbs & mingles with the whole

The work is done!—Nor folly's active rage,
Nor envy's self shall blot the golden page
Time shall admire, his mellowing hand employ
And mend the immortal tablet not destroy—

By an invariable Law of the Animal Economy, pressure on a part produces its absorption.
Townsand[29]

Beaumont's Medical Notebook

Hippocrates says, "Past things must be learnt, present known, & things future foretold"—Van Swieten[30]

If" says Hippocrates on administering cathartic medicines "the humors be voided which ought to be carried off, the patient will be relieved & easily bear the discharge; but if not the contrary effect will follow——

the same[31]

Van Swieten says "We know not what may be the Idea of the best Physicians in future times; but he is reckoned a good Physician, who makes use of all the assistance by which, thr° the happiness of the present age, the art of Physic has been improved—[32]

"Steel" Says Van Swieten "desolved in the milder acids is commonly preferable to all other tonics; because it acts not only by its austere astringent virtu but, because by the wonderful stimulus of its metalic sulphur, which is so friendly to our nature, it raises the vital powers" hence may we not infer that *Oxygen* is this wonderful stimulus although unknown under that name to the Chimist or Physicians of that age—at least I think it concides with the modern principles, Chemistry & Phiseology that Oxigen is the principal cause of Animal heat & vitality in the system—[33]

Van Swieten says "There are three symtoms only observed which are common to all fevers, (viz) a shivering, a quick pulse, & heat"—[34]

"Vomits should not be given, where there is just reason to suspect an inflamation of the Stomach or any other of the adjacent viscera"
    Perhaps there may be a reasonable objection to the above rule in some cases—

Huxham,[35] speaking of an Epidemic *Peripnumony*, that appear'd in the latter part of the years 1745-6—Says "after a second bleeding (& even sometimes after a single bleeding), the pulse & strength of the patients sunk to a surprising degree; & they ran into a sort of nervous fever, with great tremor, Subsultus Tendinum, profuse sweats, or an atra-bilious diarrhoea, with a black tongue, *coma*, or Delirium, tho' at the beginning the Pulse seem'd to be full & throbbing, & the pain, cough, & oppression so very urgint, as to indicate bleeding pretty strongly.

In these cases, the blood was seldom found *buffy*, to any considerable degree, but commonly very florid, but of a very loos & soft consistancy, or very dark coloured & coated with a very thin bluish or green film, under which was a soft greenish jelly, & a dark livid cruor at the bottom" &c &c In which cases, he says he is "very cautious how he advises further bleeding, especially if the Pulse, or Patient become more languid after it

Huxham[36] says "It is certain from the best observations, that in some constitutions of the *Air*, Patients under Pluritic Diseases, will not bear the loss of much blood, particularly in continued wet foggy weather: In general we find they sustain the loss with much better effect, & less inconvenience, in a cold dry spring than in a wet summer, or rainy autum—The reasons are obvious—

Brown,[37] speaking of the *Croup*—or *cynanche stridula* says, "consider what symtoms precede or accompany it, whether of strength or of debility, whether the pyrexia be sthenic or asthenic,—weigh the different opinions of authors on the subject,—suspect their theories but their *facts* still more—

Be on guard not to be misled by the vanity, emtiness, & rashness of young Physicians; as well as by the obstinacy & bigotry of the older sort, that increase with their age & practice; to be bent, by no force of reasoning, no weight of truth, scarce by the power of *God*.—Regard their minds as bound in the fetters of prejudice: Remember, that a whole age of Physicians were in the wrong, except one man (Sydenham) &

Beaumont's Medical Notebook

presisted obstinately in their error in the case of the Alixipharmac Physicians—

Sal Satyricum, This is very useful for seasoning speeches

Oleum Sycophantinum
This is a most powerful medicine—

Balsamum Soporificum—or quitting Balsam—This is sovreign for blunting the stings of conscience, the thorns of remorse, & pangs of recollection—

Opium, has the power of rendering a person surprisingly sprightly, lively, & vigilint; it begets confidence, banishes melancholy, converts fear into boldness, makes silent eloquent & silent brave.

Of all the lessons which a young man entering upon the profession of Medicine, needs to learn, this is, perhaps, the first—that he should resist the fascinations of doctrines & hypotheses, till he have won the privilege of such Studies by honest labour, & a faithful pursuit of real & useful knowledge—Of this knowledge, surely Anatomy forms the greatest share, as being the basis of all medical skill—

J. B.—P 8—[38]

Characteristical signs   Brun

α ......Stimulus in general
β ......Universal Stimulus
γ ......Local Stimulus
δ ......Bland & insipid food
ε ......Vegetable food
ζ ......Evacuants—Emt & Cath
η ......Sedatives—
θ ......Cold—
ι ......General exciting powers—
κ ......Excitability—
λ ......Sensibility—
μ ......Simple Solids
ν ......Disease & Death—

Beaumont's Medical Notebook

Aetiology.
Doctrine of remote causes

ξ ......Excitement—
ο ......The stimulus of Spiritous liquids
π ...... "   "   " Musk
ρ ......{Volatile Alkali / Either & Opium} {the highest & most difusible in the inverted order in which they stand—}
τ ......Improper aliment
ς ......Volatile Alkali
υ ......Aether—
φ ......Opium—
χ ......Penery of blood
ψ ......Direct debility
ω ......Indirect debility
Α ......Evacuations in General
Β ......Secerning System
Γ ......Gestation
Δ ......Exercise
Ε ......Contagious Matter
Ζ ......Poisons
Η ......Inflamation
Θ ......Sthenic Diseases
Κ ......Premature Sleep
Λ ......Morbid Sleep
Μ ......Passion—
Ν ......Watching

Convenienter Naturæ
Agreeable to Nature

Mix Sal. Ammon & Snow & whilst they are melting over a fire, a bowl of water may be congeal'd by being set into it.—

"To distinguish general diseases from local ones, the following marks are to be understood. 1st their being preceded by a diathesis, & this followed by one similar to it,—while on the contrary local affections are distinguished 1st by the affection

[23]

of a part & by the abscence of a diathesis or only its accidental presence—

In order to attain this useful knowledge, we must learn what is necessary from anatomy, waste no time in superfluous study in it, dissect subjects; distinguish remaining effects from causes that have passed away; examine diligently very many bodies of persons who have been hanged, drowned, died of wounds, &c; compare these diligently with bodies of those who have died by lingering & often repeated disease; compare every particular with the whole; guard against the rashness of forming opinions, & if you can, you will be among a very few, who have ever been able to do so; never expect to discover the cause of disease *in dead bodies*; be circumspect in forming a judgment"

Brun[39]

Riches are oft' by guilt & business earn'd;
Or dealt by chance, to shield a lucky knave,
Or throw a fairer sunshine on a fool,
Armstrong[40]

A question? Is it lawful or justifiable to take away one persons life, for the preservation of another's?

J—— May she, with all her Farrago of falshood, detraction & malice sink by the weight of her own wickedness into eternal infamy—

Opinions of Various Authors, respecting the Doctrine of Fevers Of Cullen,[41] Whose whole Doctrine of Fevers is explicitly this.

The remote causes are certain, sedative powers applied to the nervous system, which diminishing the energy of the brain thereby producing debility in the whole of the functions & particularly in the action of the extreme vessels. Su[c]h, however, is at the same time that the nature of the Animal economy, that this debility proves an indirect stimulus to the sanguiferous system, whince by the intervention of the cold stage & the spasm connected with it, the action of the heart & larger arteries are increased & continue so till it has had the effect of restoring the energy of the brain, of extending this energy to the extreme vessels, of restoring therefore their action & thereby especially overcoming the spasm effecting them the removing of which, the exertion of sweat, & other marks of relaxation of excretoins take place—

Sydenham,[42] speaking of the cause of acute epidimic diseases, Says, "some of them proceed from a latent, & inexplicable alteration of the air, infecting the bodies of men, & not from any peculiar state of disposition of blood & juices, any farther than an occult influence of the air may communicate this to the body: These continue only during this one secret state or constitution of the air & raging at no other time are called epidemic distempers—

Physicians, when tending upon their patients, should make their health their first object: So gentle & sympathizing should be their dispositions & manner in the apartment of the sick, that pain & distress should seem suspended in their presence. So exhilerating ought their visits to be, that Hope should follow their footsteps, or so salutary their prescriptions, that *Death* should drop his commission in combat with their skill—

Washington—His name immortalized on Earth——May his transcendant virtues, wisdom & integrity, be engraven in indeleable characters, on the hearts of true American, the wellwisher to his country, the true friend of her liberties, & zealous supporter of her Independance—May the Laurel of victory ever flourish on the grave of departed worth—& surviving Patriots & Heroes live to reap the fruit of his blessed labours in their unparallelled fame——May the canvass, paper & clay—bear the glorious image of his person, the sacred remembrance of his precepts, & the most solemn reverence to his godlike examples, to ages yet unborn—

Motus Abnormis $\begin{cases} \text{an unnatural motion of} \\ \text{Intestines or any other part} \end{cases}$
Post-Mortem—After death

Beaumont's Medical Notebook

Commenc'd duty as Surg's Mate in the 6th Reg[t] Infty on Brevet from Gen[l] Bloomfield,[43] Sep[t] 13, 1812
—Rec[d] notice of an appointment in the 16th Infty. on the 12th De[cr]—Suspended duty 1st of Jan[y]—1813—
—Rec[d] Transfer to the 6th & recommenced duty 15th Feb[y]. 1813—
Rec[d] pay up to the 31st De[cr] 1812
Rec[d] commission as Mate about the 10th of March 1813—
 Rec[d] pay to the 28th Feb[y]. 1813
  " " " " 30th June 1813

Cases[44] Mrs. Polly, wife of Mr. *C. Huntre*, of a slender constitution & cold, phlegmatic habit—married in May 1816 was happily delivered of a fine large healthy boy on the 15th of Feby. 1817 —remained very comfortable for 5 or 4 hours had a refreshing sleep, & awoke free from pain or disagreeable sensation

 But in the course of half an hour complained of a pain at the pit of the Stomach which she supposed to be merely flatus, & took a small dose of Elix Paregoric & Es. Pip. Minth. without any essential relief—the pain continued to increase rapidly—a violent reching & puking ensued—rejecting monstrous foeatid black bilious matter, by spontaneous efforts—without any relief—In an hour after the commencement of the distress judging from the matter rejected that an Emetic of Ipecac & Sulph-Iron indicated—I gave a gentle one which had a kind operation & seemed to give momentary relief—but no permanent effect—although it evacuated much foul bilious matter— yet in a short time she relapsed into the same condition, & was most violently seized with spasams of the most alarming nature—which left her in the space of a minute deprived of her reason or recollection—these spasams, recurred at irregular intervals—for about 72 hours—but with the same invariable symtoms—the first appearance of a recurrence, was an apparent revival of strength & diminution of pain—then the eye lids would seem to rise involuntarily, the eyes moderately moving with more than common lustar for a few seconds— then a frequent winking—with the Eyes moving to the left— the muscles of the mouth & face beginning to twitch, drawing mostly to the left, a horrid distortion of the whole features—

terminating in a general & violent—convulsion followed by great difficulty of respiration & sense of sufocation—ending, in a great prostation of strength—turgessency of the countenance—& frothing at the mouth—leaving the patient in a comatose state untill the recurence of a succeeding fit, which at first occured one in about 15 minutes—afterwards not so often—sometimes leaving an interval of 2 or 3 hours, & then returning with more violence—& so continued untill relief could be obtained from the operation of medicine which was not under 48 hours—

The most powerful antispasmodics were liberally administered in vain—no relief could be observed, not even in *arresting* the spasams, by large doses of opium, Castor,[45] Aether, Amber &c the warm bath & friction & injections were all useless in preventing or even relieving the convulsions for 36 hours—when by the administration & operation of about *eight grains* of *Cal* & three grains of musk. evry 2 hours—blisters upon the extremeties, a large one on the abdomen, & the use of stimulating injections, a copious discharge of most foeatid bilious matter from her bowels gave the first signs of rescuing her from death—Forty hours after the attack she experienced the first relief from the operation of the above mentioned treatment—& continued to be reliev'd by the use of the *cal musk.* in smaller portions—with the addition of camphor, & Ipecac repeated evry 4 hours,—keeping up a discharge from the bowels daily by the use of *Ol Ricini—Salts*, Senna, manna & mag *Alb* not omitting frequent Injections of an Infus^n of Salts Senna—alternated with yeast or Broth—giving, for nourishment Arrowroot, with small q^{ty} of wine—chicken broth &c under the foregoing treatment she recovered rapidly & in the space of 4 weeks was able to ride a mile or two & in 5 or 6 commenced her domestic duties again—NB. One thing merits noticing in this case—in particular, that is, she lost all recollection & sense of reason from the first fit & what is still more singular when she began to regain her reason—could not recollect any, not even the most important circumstances of her life for more than a year last past, & as she slowly regained her strength, & reason she came gradually to her recollection—recognizing faintly the most distant & important events subsequent to her being married & so she continues to recover her recollection in the same ratio as she regains her health & strength—acting, as it were, the scene of the last year of her life over again—

Robert Burns says he "Believes there is no holding converse, or carrying on correspondence, with an amiable fine woman, without some mixture of that most delicious passion, whose most devoted slave I have more than once had the honor of being: but why be hurt or offended on that account? Can no honest man have a prepossession for a fine woman, but he must run his head against an intrigue? Take a little of the tender witchraft of Love, & add to it the generous, the honorable sentiments of manly friendship; & I know but *one* more delightful morsal which few, few in any rank ever taste—Such a composition is like adding cream to strawberries—it not only gives the fruit a more elegant richness, but has a peculiar deliciousness of its own—

Reliques of *Rob Burns*[46]
358

Coarse minds are not aware how much they injure the keenly-feeling tie of bosom friendship, when in their foolish officiousness, they mention what nobody cares for recollecting. People of nice sensibility, & generous minds, have a certain intrinsic dignity, that fires at being trifled with, or lowered, or even too nearly approached—Burns[47]
To be feelingly alive to kindness & to unkindness, is a charming female character—

Rqs. of R. Burns
365

I have a little infirmity in my disposition, that where I fondly *love* or highly esteem, I cannot bear reproach—

R.R.B.
365

A decent means of livelihood in the world, an approving *God*, a peaceful conscience & one firm, trusty friend! can any body that has these, be said to be unhappy? Rqs. RB
366

How wretched is the condition of one who is haunted with conscious guilt—& trembling under the idea of dreaded vengeance! & what a placid what a charming secret enjoyment—it gives, to bosom the kind feelings of friendship & the fond throes of love! Out upon the tempest of anger, the acrimonious gall of fretful impatience, the sullen frost of lowering resentment, or the corroding poison of withered envy! They eat up the immortal part of man!

If they spent their fury only on the unfortunate objects of theirs, it would be something in their favor; but these miserable passions, like *traitor* Iscariot, betray their Lord & master—
Rqs R B.
368

Shaw, a private soldier in Capt. B. K. Pierce's[48] compy. U. S. Art^y. was struck with a heavy club over the head, which blow depressed a portion of the os front. on the left side about ¼ of an inch, fracturing, (or rather, producing a fishure) in the inner table of the skull running from the frontal sinus obliquely toward the corronal angle of the parietal bone—

The injury was done on the morning of the 7th Decr. 1820—he appeared stupid from that time—would walk about when compelled—but said nothing, except *yes & no* occasionally—looked wild with his Eyes, & these frequently seem'd obliquely fixed towards the right side—complained of nothing—continued in this condition 24 hours—when he was attacked with severe spasms—commencing in his Eyes, *mouth & mussles of the face*—drawing to the right *side invariably*, & extending to the head, neck & breast—& sometimes became universal & violent over the whole system—but most so upon the right side—the left appearing rather paralytic than otherwise—this is the appearance exhibited the first time I saw him which was six days after the injury was rec^d & he had then been bro^t 15 or 10 miles through the snow & cold on a train[49] & was wet & chilled thro—on examination found marks of a heavy blow upon the os frontis—considerable contusion & extravasation of blood about the left Eye, but no evident fracture or depression—his Extremeties cold—spasms every 10 or 15 minutes—severe & increasing—comatose—insensible—loss of muscular motion—laborious breathing—& small pulse—Eyes half open—rolling & insensible to the Stimulus of light—In this situation I rec^d him into the Hosp^l. 13th Decr. had him immediately washed all over in warm soap suds & ribbed with warm camp^d spts—gave him Eather—Laud^m. & Spts ammonia & warm inf^n of valerian & Castor for 2 or 3 hrs. to restore the action of the extreme vessels & raise the circulation—this done—I opened a vein & took 10—or 12. oz blood which gave very slight relief—I then administred 10 grs Cal & 5 valerian, twice repeated—followed by a Cath^c injection—produced several free stools—spasms continued to increase in frequency & form for 18 hours—finding no probability of radical relief from medical means—I throught it advisable to purforate the cranium, under the belief that extravesated fluids were diffused upon the brain—& required to be discharged—although there was no fracture, or even evident depression to be discoverd external of the integuments—yet yet presuming from the direction of the blow & the appearance of the contusion, it must be beneath the frontal bone of the side injured—I mad a cranial incision over this & on dissecting found an evident depression of the skull ⅛ inch—applied the trephine about the center of the bone—2 inches above the frontal sinous & on taking out the circular piece found a fishure extending exactly across its center in a direction from the sinous towards the coronal angle of the left parietal bone—a quantity of dark, grumous blood oozed from the incession of the Saw as it cut through & much more discharged by depressing the dura mater & elevating the depressed portion—

 The spasms continued during the operation with unabated force & frequency & for 12 hours after—they then became less frequent but equally hard—The side opposite the injury was most effected by spasms—Operation perform'd between 3 & 4 OK P.M. 12th—gave him an Inf n of val & Castor, through the night—Spasms continud to diminish in frequency

13th Spasms continued thr° the night, but less frequent & equally hard—other variation of symtoms—Sweat profusely—passed his water freely—Tongue typhoid—countenance cadaverous—removed the superficial dressing & cleansed the wound—did not look very bad—filled it with Carbon[50]—& applied the Carbon poultice on the whole—rubbed al over warm soap suds & Camp d spts—Administered Spts Mindereri[51] (Ag. Carb. Am.) & soluble Tarter. tablespoonful every 2 hrs. alternately—Arrow root & Gruel for diet—Spasms much less frequent & diminished in force this evening—tongue moist—pulse sinking—symtoms less favorable—7 OK P.M.

14th continues sinking—Spasms less, in force & frequency—as nature expires—every remedy ineffectual—Died 14th Decem—6 OK P.M.—3 hours after demise—opened & examined head—found a fracture about 5 inches long extending from within about half an inch of the center of the os. frontis, running obliquely towards the base of the Ear—with two short transverse fractures, running in a direction towards the coronal angle of the parietal bone across which I cut with the circular saw as mentioned in the operation—The depression was even & very slight—the extravasation was extensive, both external & internal of the *dura mater*—firm adhesion had taken place between the Dura mater & brain al over the left hemisphere—Suppuration had formed an abscess in about the center of the left lobe of the Cerebrum—a large quantity of grumous & extravasated blood was diffused between the *dura & pia mater* throughout the left hemisphere. The right hemisphere was sound & healthy—

Beaumont's Medical Notebook

[*Beginning in back of notebook*:]

Prescriptions   Formulae   Pilula partes aequales   [This line
                           P Æ   crossed out]
Gm Gamboge... ʒ fs   Gm Gamboge
Gm Aloes...... ʒ fs   " Aloes
Gm Scammon... ʒ fs   " Scammon
Sapo Casteel.... ʒij   Sapo Casteel
Ant. Panacea[52].. ʒij Ant. Panca   Copa.
                        Q.S.M.F.P.S.A.   Bals
Bals. Copivi..... Q.S.M.F.P.S.A.   Mis. Fiat
              Chandler[53]———

Fel Bovis[54]   Equal parts. Bovis. Sapo. Casteel
                         & Sal. Mart.[55] with Bals. Copa.
Corrector Digestiva   Q.S.M.F.P.S.A.
                                    Chandler

Anti Dysint
    Two parts. Gm Opi—
    Three parts. Ipecac
    Five parts. Sapo. Cast.
    Bals Copavia. Q.S.M.F.P.S.A.
                        Powell[56]

Equal parts. Rhie, Scammony, & Call. & as much D.R. Sugar as is equal to the whole reduced to fine powder, taken in doses of ʒi once in 2 or 3 days—

Fel Bovis   ʒij
Sapo Cast.   ʒiij
Sal. Mart.   ʒiij
M F Pillulae—
              Chandler

[32]

Beaumont's Medical Notebook

Aqua Opthalmia
P Æ, Partes Æquales—Sal. Mart. ʒ ſs
    "   "   Nit. Alb.   "
    "   "   Gum Opii "
                  One pint water

---

*Q*uantum *S*ufficit, *M*ake a mixture, mist or misce *F*iat let it then be *made* into *S*olution *S*ecundum *A*rtem——

Take ʒ 1 ſs Nitrous Acid, with 6 gills water—daily—
Syphilistic   M.E. Vol. V, P. 402.[57]

Oxygenated Muriat of Potas given from 4 to 8 grs four times a day, to begin with, though when carried to 15 or 16, has been found effectual in Lues Venersie.

                      50
℞ Acid. Vitriol   gtt. 10   for Psora
   Aqua Ros.   gtt. 20
   Axung Porcin—ʒj
   Essent Citri   gtt. 15
       M. f. Liniment. M. et V. utend.
                                 Townsand[58]

Hippocrates says "Past things must be learnt, present known, & things future foretold"[59]

℞ Fo Indeleable Ink
   Nitrat of Silver   ʒiiij
   Rain Water   ʒiiij
let it stand till clear, then add to it 60 Drops of
Solution of Nut Galls.—{ ʒij Pulvs
                           { to 1 Gill water

℞. for fire & water proof *Cement*
   Take milk & vinegar āā ½ pt. Separate the curd from the whey & mix with the whey, the whites of 3 or 4 eggs, beating the whole well together—when well mixed, add a little quick-lime through a sieve untill it have acquired the consistancy of thick paste—for cracked or broken earthen

[33]

Notes—PART I

[1] Albrecht von Haller, *First Lines of Physiology*. Chapter XVII—Internal Senses. In the first American edition, Troy 1803, the passage is on pp. 274-275.

[2] Methodus Medendi.

[3] Bread crumbs boiled to a pulp in milk, broth, or water and then flavored.

[4] William Saunders, *A Treatise on the Structure, Oeconomy and Diseases of the Liver; Together with an Inquiry into the Properties and Component Parts of the Bile and Biliary Concretions*. First edition, London, 1793.

[5] Consisted of powder of ipecacuanha and opium.

[6] Serpentaria: Virginia snakeroot.

[7] The following recipe is given for Alterative Pills in *Formulae Selectae*, New York, 1818; p. 82:

℞ Gum. Guaiac. Off.   ʒij.
   Sulphuret. Antim. Praecip.   ʒi.
   Sub-Mur. Hydrarg.   gr. viij.
   Syrup. Simp.   q. s. M.
Divide into pills LX.

[8] Brown's Sthenic Pill in *Formulae Selectae, loc. cit.*, p. 64:

℞ Sulph. Stibiat. Fusc.   gr. xv.
   Gum. Opii.
   Sub-Mur. Hydrarg.   aa   gr. x.
   Bal. Myrox. Peruif.   q. s. M.
Make into pills of gr. i. each.

[9] For a detailed discussion of the diseases in the campaign of 1812 on the northern frontier see James Mann, *Medical Sketches of the Campaigns of* 1812, 13, 14, Dedham, 1816, pp. 11-46.

[10] On November 16, 3,000 regulars and 2,000 militia, commanded by Gen. Henry Dearborn, advanced to the outposts of Lacolle, Quebec. On November 20 before daybreak the "attack" was begun. After a half hour of firing it was discovered that two American forces were firing on each other! Five men were killed and five wounded. Immediately afterwards the troops were removed to Plattsburg. *Cf.* Walter Hill Crockett, *A History of Lake Champlain*, Burlington, Vt., 1909, p. 239.

[11] During the winter of 1812 the army did not provide woolen shirts for its soldiers, but the following winter they became a part of the equipment. Mann, *op. cit.*, pp. 39-41.

[12] *Cf. infra* p. 32 for prescription.

[13] Samuel Gilliland, from Pennsylvania, commissioned May 15, 1812, disbanded June 1815. Harvey E. Brown, *The Medical Department of the United States Army from 1775 to 1873*, Washington, 1873, p. 268.

[14] *Cf.* Beaumont's other notebook p. 43 *infra* where he explains his suspension of duty "on account of the unfavorable prospects of the army at that time" and returned to Plattsburg to sound out the possibilities of beginning private practice there.

[15] Probably James H. Bradford, from Massachusetts, appointed Surgeon's Mate in 9th Inf. 14 April 1812, promoted to Surgeon, Third Artillery, Oct. 1813. *Cf.* Brown, *op. cit.*, p. 276.

[16] Tincture.

[17] For a more detailed account of the journey see pp. 43-44 *infra*.

[18] Although Beaumont does not mention it, Mann reported that 20 men of General Pike's brigade suffered badly frozen toes and feet, nearly all of which required amputation. Mann, *op. cit.*, p. 57.

[19] This port at the eastern end of Lake Ontario in New York state had been the winter refuge of the American fleet when the frozen lakes prevented operations against the enemy. It was protected by two batteries and two block-houses.

[20] Calomel.

[21] Now Toronto. For a detailed account of the battle of York see Beaumont's second notebook pp. 45-48 *infra*, and also Mann, *op. cit.*, pp. 58-59.

[22] Upper Canada.

[23] John Moncure Daniel (1769-1813), born in Stafford County, Virginia, studied in

[34]

Notes—Part I

Scotland, entered the U. S. Army medical service in 1809 with the appointment of Hospital Surgeon. W. B. Blanton, *Medicine in Virginia in the Nineteenth Century*, Richmond, Va., 1933, p. 363.

[24] Joseph Lovell (1788-1836) of Boston, Mass., who in 1818 became the first Surgeon General of the U. S. Army. Early in this war he distinguished himself through his efficient administration of the general hospital at Burlington, Vt., which was a model of cleanliness and order. He remained a lifelong friend of Beaumont and encouraged him in his subsequent experiments on the gastric juice.

[25] The text ends abruptly at the bottom of a page, indicating that some leaves of the notebook have been lost. The following quotations and excerpts from reading to page 25 were probably written while Beaumont was still a student, and are contemporaneous with pp. 1-9.

[26] By Isaac Watts (1674-1748) in *The Psalms of David Imitated in the Language of the New Testament, and apply'd to the Christian State and Worship*, London, 1719, No. 420. *Cf.* John Julian, *A Dictionary of Hymnology*, Revised Edition, London, 1925.

[27] Edward Young (1683-1765), *Night Thoughts* 4:667.

[28] Sylvius, or Franciscus de la Boe (1614-1672), an outstanding Leyden professor who made important advances in physiological chemistry. As his name here has no connection with the rest of the text, Beaumont had probably simply jotted it down in order to remember it.

[29] Joseph Townsend, *Elements of Therapeutics; or a Guide to Health; Being Cautions and Directions in the Treatment of Diseases.* Designed chiefly for the use of students. First American edition, Boston, 1802.

[30] *Cf.* Schomberg, *Van Swieten's Commentaries Abridged*, London, 1762, p. 17. This passage must have especially impressed Beaumont, as he repeats it on p. 33.

[31] *Ibid.*, p. 12.
[32] *Ibid.*
[33] *Ibid.*, p. 23.
[34] *Ibid.*, p. 191.

[35] John Huxham, *An Essay on Fevers.* Third edition, London, 1757, pp. 184-185.

[36] *Ibid.*, pp. 256-257.

[37] John Brown, *The Elements of Medicine*, Vol. II, London, 1788, pp. 100-101.

[38] This passage and the following table is undoubtedly from some edition of Brown's *Elements*, although I was not able to locate it. Brun here and later refers to the Latinized form of Brown's name: Bruno.

[39] In the edition of Brown, Philadelphia, 1791, this passage stands in Vol. I, p. 31.

[40] John Armstrong, *The Art of Preserving Health*, Book IV: 289-291. The same lines are also copied in the other notebook, *cf.* p. 39 *infra*.

[41] William Cullen (1710-1790), Professor of Medicine at Edinburgh, whose text-book *First Lines of the Practice of Physick*, first published London, 1777, was widely used.

[42] *Cf. The Works of Thomas Sydenham, M.D., on Acute and Chronic Diseases; with Their Histories and Modes of Cure.* With notes... by Benjamin Rush, M.D., Philadelphia, 1809, p. 2.

[43] General Joseph Bloomfield. By September 1 he had assembled an army of 8,000 men on the west shore of Lake Champlain.

[44] At this time Beaumont was engaged in private practice at Plattsburg, having returned there in 1815 after resigning from the Army.

[45] A bitter orange-brown substance with a penetrating odor found in two sacs between the anus and external genitalia of the beaver, used as a stimulant and antispasmodic.

[46] *Reliques of Robert Burns; consisting chiefly of original Letters, Poems, and Critical Observations on Scottish Songs.* Collected and Published by R. H. Cromek. London, T. Cadell & W. Davies, 1808.

[47] *Ibid.*, p. 364.

[48] This case occurred shortly after Beaumont had begun his duties as Post Surgeon at Fort Mackinac. Captain B. K. Pierce, the commanding officer of the fort, was the brother of President Franklin Pierce.

Notes — Part I

[49] A long heavy sleigh used to transport merchandise, wood, etc.

[50] Charcoal.

[51] An aqueous solution of ammonium acetate, used as a diaphoretic, named for R. M. Minderer (c. 1570-1621) of Augsburg who discovered it.

[52] Recipe as follows:

> Take of Antimony, six ounces;
> Nitre, two ounces;
> Common salt, one ounce and an half;
> Charcoal, an ounce.
> All heated in a crucible.

Cf. James Thacher, *The American New Dispensatory*, Boston, 1810, p. 281.

[53] Undoubtedly Dr. Benjamin Chandler, his teacher.

[54] Ox-gall.

[55] Ferrous sulphate.

[56] Probably Dr. Truman Powell (1776-1841), a Burlington, Vt., physician from whom Beaumont obtained a testimonial on Sept. 10, 1812. Cf. Jesse S. Myer, *Life and Letters of Dr. William Beaumont*, St. Louis, 1912, p. 31.

[57] This notation and the following are from Robert John Thornton, *The Philosophy of Medicine: or, Medical Extracts on the Nature of Health and Disease* . . . Fourth edition, London, 1800.

[58] Cf. Townsend, op. cit., p. 591.

[59] Repetition of quotation on p. 20.

[36]

Wm. BEAUMONT's
FORMATIVE YEARS

Two Early Notebooks
1811-1821

Part II

THE ERIE CANAL

PART II
Beaumont's General Notebook
Literary excerpts.
War and travel diaries.

Peter's Apology, for leaving his
Wife, to go into the Country awhile[1]

Chloe, we must not always be in heaven,
   Forever, toying, ogling, kissing, billing;
The joys for which, I, thousands would have giv'n
   Will presently, be scarcely worth a shilling.

Thy neck is fairer than the Alpine snows,
   And s[w]eetly swelling, beats the down of doves;
Thy cheek of health, a rival to the rose;
   Thy pouting lips the throne of all the loves;
Yet, though thus beautiful beyond expression,
That beauty fadeth, by too much possession—
Economy in love is peace to Nature,
Much like, economy in worldly matter:
We should be prudent, never live too fast;
Profusion willnot, cannot always last—
Lovers are really spendthrifts—'tis a shame—
Nothing their thoughtless wild career can tame,
   Till pen'ry stares them in the face,
And when they find an empty purse,
Grow calmer, wiser, how their fault they curse,
And, limping look with such a sneering grace;
Job's war-horse fierce, his neck with thunder hung
Sunk to a humble hack that carries dung—
Smell to the queen of flow'rs, the fragrant rose,—
Smell twenty times—& thin [then], my dear, the nose,

Will tell thee (not so much for scent athirst)
The twentieth drank less flavor than the first—
   Love, doubtless is the sweetest of all fellows;
Yet often should the little God retire—
Abscence, dear Chloe, is a pair of bellows
That keeps alive the sacred fire—

*   *   *

THE HAPPY PAIR

Here beneath my humble cot,
Tranquil peace & pleasure dwell,
If contented with our lot,
Smiling joy can grace a cell—

Nature's wants are all suppli'd;
Food & raiment, house & fire:
Let others swell the courts of Pride,
This is all that I require—

*   *   *

Social Affection.[2] Is the mildest & most agreeable of all mental stimuli— It sweetens ev'ry bitter of life— It is able alone, to support the drooping mind, whin the sorrows of a wounded heart want vent—When the noble'st endeavours are rejected, when the sacred impuls of conscious truth ridiculeed, & hissed at, & despised, the tear of sorrow is wiped away by the gentle, tender & affectionate addresses of a female mind, who has an aspect like that of unpracticed, cloistered virginity, which feels & is able to efface each emotion, each passion, in the most concealed feature of her husbands countenance, & by endearing means, without what the world calls beauty, shines forth in countenance, heavenly as an angel—

Sweat is the breath of morn, her rising sweet,
With charm of earliest birds: pleasan the sun
When first on this delightful land he spreads
His orient beams, on herb, trees, fruit, & flow'er,
Glist'ning with dew; fragrant the fertile earth
After soft show'ers; & sweet the coming on

Beaumont's General Notebook

Of grateful evening mild: thin [then] silent night
With this hir solemn bird of night; & this fair moon,
And these the gems of heav'n, her starry train—
But neither breath of morn, when she ascends
With charm of earliest birds: nor herb, fruit, flowr—
Glist'ning with dew: nor fragrance after showers:
Nor grateful evening mild: nor silint night,
With this her solemn bird: nor walk by moon;
Or glitt'ring star-light, without thee is sweet.   Th[ton].3

Virtue, the strength & beauty of the soul,
It pleases & it lasts;—a happiness
That even above the smiles & frowns of fate
Exalts great Nature's favorites: a wealth
That ne'er encumbers, nor to baser hands
Can be transfer'd: it is the only good
Man justly boasts of, or can call *his own*.
Riches are oft by guilt or baseness earn'd;
Or dealt by chance, to shield a lucky knave,
Or throw a fairer sunshine on a fool—
But for one end, one much neglected use,
Are riches worth your care (for Nature's wants
Are few, & without opulence suppli'ed)
This noble end is, to produce the soul;
To shew the virtues in their fairest light;
To make humanity the minister
Of bounteous Providence; & teach the breast
That *generous luxury*, the good enjoy.
Oh! blest of heav'n, whom not the languid songs
Of luxury, not the inviting bribes
Of sordid wealth, nor all the gaudy spoils
Of pageant honors can seduce to leave
Those ever blooming sweets, which from the store
Of Nature fair imagination culls
To charm the enliv'ning soul! For him, the spring
Distills her dews, & from the silken gems
It[s] lucid leaves unfolds: for him, the hand
Of Autumn tinges evry fertile branch

[39]

Beaumont's General Notebook

With blooming gold, & blushes like the morn.
Each passing hour sheds tribute from her wings;
And still new beauties meet *his* lonely walk,
And loves unfelt attract him. Not a breeze
Flies o'er the meadow, not a cloud imbibes
The setting sun's effulgence, not a strain
From all the tenants of the warbling shade
Ascends, but whin his bosom can partake
Frish pleasure, unreprov'd.—Or whin lightning's fire
The Arch of heav'n, & thunders rock the ground;
Whin furious whirlwinds rend the howling air,
And Ocean, groaning from the lowest bed,
Heaves his tempestuous billows to the sky:
Amid the mighty uproar, while below
The Nations tremble, he, *good man*, looks abroad
From some high cliff, superior, & enjoys
The elemantal war—
                                    Armstrong[4]

THE ADVANTAGES OF A CULTIVATED MIND

Such are the charms to barren states assign'd,
Their wants but few, their wishes all confin'd.
Yet let them only share the praises due;
If few their wants, their pleasures are but few,
For ev'ry want that stimulates the breast,
Becomes a source of pleasure when redrest.
Whence from such lands each pleasing science flies,
That first excites desire, & then supplies;
Unknown to them, when sensual pleasures cloy,
To fill the languid pause with finer joy;
Unknown those powers that raise the soul to flame,
Catch ev'ry nerve & vibrate thr° the frame,
Their level life is but a mould'ring fire,
Unquench'd by want, unfan'd by strong desire;
Unfit for raptures; or if raptures cheer,
On some high festival of once a year,
In wild excess the vulgar breast takes fire,
Till, buried in debauch, the bliss expire—   Th[ntn 5]

[40]

View of Plattsburg.

THE UNITED STATES HOTEL, PLATTSBURG, N. Y.
Owned by Israel Green, Beaumont's future father-in-law.

Beaumont's General Notebook

OF AMBITION[6]

Sweet is the concord of harmonious sounds,
Whin the soft lute or pealing organ strikes
The well-attemper'd ear; sweet is thé breath
Of honest love, whin nymph & gentle swain
Waft sighs alternate to each other's hearts:
But not the concord of harmonious sounds,
Whin the soft lute, or pealing organ strikes
The well-attemper'd ear; nor the sweet breath
Of honest love, whin nymph & gentle swain
Waft sighs alternate to each other's heart,
So charm with ravishment the rapturd sense,
As does the voice of well deserv'd report
Strike with sweet melody the conscious soul!

Although imitation is one of the greatest instruments used by Providence in bringing our nature towards perfection, yet if men gave themselves up to imitation entirely, & each followed the other, & so on in an eternal circle it is easy to see that there never could be any improvement among them—

Man must remain as brutes do, the same at the end, as they are at this day, & that they were in the beginning of the world—

To prevent this, God has planted in man a sense of ambition, and a satisfaction arising from the contemplation of his excelling his fellows in something deemed valuable among them— It is this passion that creates advantages we all derive in civilized life, & it is this passion also, ill directed, which often unfortunately hinders men from granting to genius its due—

Thornton[7]

ON ANGER

When reason, like the skilful charioteer,
Can break the fiery passions to the bit,
And, spite of their licentious sallies keep
The radiant track of Glory; PASSIONS, then
Are aids & ornaments— *Young*—[8]

Beaumont's General Notebook

THE REWARD OF ATTENTION TO THE LAWS OF ANIMAL OECONOMY

The man who is attentive to the maxims of health, which we have before delivered,
>Will prosper like the tender reed,
Whose top waves gently o'er the mead;
And move, such blessings virtue follow
In *health*, & Beauty an Apollo—

>Like dew drops from the crystal stream,
Will his Eyes with pearly lustre beam;
And with marks of firm health o'erspread,
His cheeks surpass the morning's red—

>The fairest of the female train
For him shall bloom, nor bloom in vain
O happy she, whose lips he presses!
O happy she, whom he caresses!
>> *Thornton*[9]

Modesty—Is one of the most distinguishing & attractive characteristics of the female sex.

Modesty has a double effect: it heightins the desire of the male & deters him from rudeness, or improper behavuour. It both *attracts & repels*. There is no part of the female character which men so much revere as *modesty*— It is the brightest & most valuable jewel with which a woman can be adorned.

A fine woman without *modesty* instead of gaining the affections of men, becomes an object of contempt—

It is, therefore, not only the interest of females to cultivate *modesty*; but to guard with the most anxious attention, against the smallest encroachments. Ev'ry attack, however apparently insignificant, should be repelled with spirit & intrepidity. To men of sensibility, a single glance of the Eye will tell them that their conduct is improper & make them not only instantly desist, but prevent any further attempt—

It is equally the Interest of men to cherish, & not to injure

Beaumont's General Notebook

by indelicacy a quality from which they derive so much pleasure & advantage—

> Hail Modesty! fair female honor, hail!
> Beauty's *chief ornament*, without whose charms
> Beauty disgusts; or gives but vulgar joys.—
> Cheapness offends; hence on the harlots lips
> No rapture hangs, however fair she seems,
> However form'd for love & amorous play.—
> Thou giv'st the smile its grace; the heighten'd kiss
> Its balmy essence sweet! &c——
> Armstrong

On candid reflection, one must readily conclude, *with Sydenham*, that to assist mankind by curing their diseases & repairing their constitutions, is preferable to being commended by them, & highly conducive to tranquility of mind, popular, applause being lighter than a feather, or a bubble & less substantial than a dream—[10]

1812 Sept 8th Quit my Precepter, Doct Benjn Chandler,[11] St Albans /Vt/ under whose friendly inspection & instruction I happily pursued my, *medical* studies, for 2 years, to my own satisfaction & that of my Preceptor—came to Plattsburgh—join'd the Army[12]—as *Surg's Mate* of the 6th Infty on the 13th Inst—continued duty as such till 1st Jany. 1813—at which piriod I suspended duty on account of the unfavorable prospects of the Army at that time & proposed to the people of Plattsburgh[13] to commence private practice in that & the neighbouring vicinities—met with good encouragement, during six weeks, in which time visitid my *respected* friends, at St Albans—

On the 15th Feby. recommenced service in 6th Infty on account of the prospects there was then of an engagement with the *Enemy*

1813

Continued in Camp Saranac[14] till 19th March, when the 1st Brig^e.[15] march'd for Sackett's-Harbour, a distance of 180 miles—passing thr^o a delightful country & many beautiful Villages &

Beaumont's General Notebook

Settlements, of which *Malon*[16] was the first after leaving Plattsburgh a very flourishing Town, situated on an excellent mill-stream, & surrounded by a fine country of land—Thince thr° Bangor, Constable, Hopkinton, all very fine Townships—to Canton—a Town very flourishing—people wealthy affording excellent accomodations to travellers—passing thr° a Town calld Governnur,[17] situated on, what is called Salmon River—not much to be admired—thence thr° several Towns, & small villages, of little note to Water Town, a very pleasant village standing on the west side of Black river, within 10 miles of the harbor it is a Shire Town,[18] & very flourishing—from thence to *Sacketts Harbour*, where we encamp, from the 27th March till our imbarkation on board the Ships, for the Enimies Shores—Sackett's Harbour is a small but very handsom & commodious harbour—the village is small irregular, & dirty—much business is carried on in the place—more especially Ship building at this time—[19]

The naval force is very respectable & quite formidable, consisting of of one Ship mounting 24 24-pounders—One Brig—18 18-pounders, 9 Schooners of 3-6-9-&12-Guns—with pilot Boats & Cutters, duly armd in addition to which is now on the stocks a frigate of 36 36-pounders—calculating to be done by the 1st June

1813

Sacketts' Harbour 20th April

The 1st Brigade with several detachments from other Corps,[20] in readiness, & waiting in suspense to embark on board the navy, for an expected attack on the enemy—Gen¹ Dearborn,[21] arriv'd in Town to night

---

21st

Weather rainy—wind southeast—Sick mending—Troops waiting for orders to embark—11 oclk—nothing remarkable has occured to day—wind south—weather rainy—11 PM—

22—

Embarked, with Capt Humphreys, Capt. Walworth & Muhlenburg,[22] & comp^y on board the *Schooner Julia*. The rest of the

SACKETT'S HARBOR IN 1814.

TORONTO IN 1813

Brigade, the 2ᵈ with Foresyths'[23] Rifle Regᵗ & the light Artillury on board the Ship, Brig, & other Schooners,—remain'd in the Harbour till next morn'g.

23. AM 11 ock—

Weigh'd Anchor, & put out, under the impression of going to Kingston[24]—got out 15, or 20 miles, came on a storm—wind a head & the fleet returnd into harbour—no one permitted to go on shore—

24—6, oc,k A.M.

Put out, of harbour, with a fair wind.—tho. mild & pleasant—the fleet sailing in fine order, affording a very pleasant scene:—

Thrᵒ the day—

25—6 ock. A.M.

Morning most delightful, Wind fresh & increasing—not fair—obliging us to beat, getting along slowly—

27— [26]

Wind pretty strong in the morning:—increasing to a strong blow so that the swells run high, tossing our vessels smartly about—Several seasick—was myself—at half past four oclock, passed by the mouth of Niagara River—this circumstance baffled our imaginations where we were going—for we were first impressed with the idea of Kingston,—thin to Niagara—but now our destination must be Little York—at Sunset came in view of York Town[25] & the Fort—where we lay off—all night with in, 3 or 4 leagues—

27—

Sail'd into harbour & came to anchor a little below the Brittish Garrison.—We now filld the boats, & affected a landing, though not without some difficulty, & the loss of some men—the Brittish, march'd their troops from the Garrison down the beach to cut us off in landing, & thᵒ they had evry advantage they could not effect their design. a hot engagement ensued in which the Enimy, lost nearly a third of their min & were soon compelled to quit the field leaving their dead & wouned strewd in evry direction—We lost but very few in the engagement.—The enemy returnd into garrison but from the loss sustain'd in the 1st engagement the undaunted courage of our min, & the brisk firing from our fleet, into the Garrison with 12 & 32 ponds [pounds] they were soon oblig^d to evacuate it & retreat with all possible speed—driven to this alternative they devised the inhuman project of blowing up their Magazine (containing 300 Bbls Powder) the explosion of which, shocking to mention, had almost, totally destroyed our Army. —above 300 were wounded, & about 60 killed dead on the spot by stones of all dimentions, falling like a shower of hail in the midst of our ranks—the Enemy had, about 20 killed & wounded by the exp^{ln} th^o the main body had retreated far out of the Garrison[26]—After this sad disaster our Army march^d into the Garrison hawl'd down the Brittish coulours (which they were too haughty to do) & raisd the American Standard on it place[27]—Our Army was about 1500 strong—Theirs about the same—Encampt in Garrison this night—mounting a guard 500 strong to secure our safty thr^o the night—A most distressing scene ensues, in the Hospital.—nothing but the Groans, of the wounded & agonies of the Dying are to be heard—The Surgeons, wading in blood, cutting of arms, legs & trepanning heads to rescue their fellow creatures from untimely deaths—to hear the poor creatures, crying—Oh, Dear! Oh Dear! Oh my God! my God! Do, Doctor, Doctor! Do cut of my leg! my arm! my head! to relieve me from misery! I cant live! I cant live! would have rent the heart of Steel, & shocked the insensibility of the most harden'd assassin & the cruelest savage! It awoke my liveliest sympathy, & I cut & slashed for 48 hours, without food or sleep—my God! who can think of the shocking scene, where his fellow creatures, lye mashed & mangled in evry part with a Leg—an Arm—a head, or a body ground in pieces without having his very heart pierced with the acutest sensibility, & his blood chill in his veins—then who can behold it without agonizing sympathy—

Beaumont's General Notebook

28—10 OCK AM

Just got time, to suspend capital opperations, whilst I can take a little refreshment to sustain life, for the first time since four oclock yesterday—return again to the bloody scene of distress to continue dressing, Amputating, & Trepaning Dressed rising of 50. patients, from simple contusions to the worst of compound fractures more than half of the last description—Perform'd two cases of Amputation, & one of Trepaning—12 ock. PM. retired to rest my much fatigued body & mind—

29—

Dress'd most of wounds over, Trepaned two, this day—ordered to get the sick wounded on board the fleet, to be transported to Sackts harbour Sent them, to the ships & the most of them were sent back again very much to the injury of the patients One of those Amputated yesterday does well, the other died in about 12 hours the fracture being in his Thigh & very much contused—

30—

Dressed, the wounded most of them doing well, the two cases of Trepaning doing well The Millitia & people giving them selves up to be paroled—nearly 1200, hundred since the 27th

May 1st—

About my professional employment, dressing the wounded, the most of them doing well—Amputated an arm—Our order for gitting all the sick & wounded on board, prevents any more opperations to day several more will have to be perform'd—The wounded on board—All the Troop ordered to embark—all on board at six ock—brought off public property, taken from his Mjestys Stores, estimated to the amt of 2000000 & a half Dolls—Burnt the ruins of the Government house the Blockhouse one or two public stores, & an old Sloop[28]

2—

Wind unfavorable to sailing out, consequently we remain in the fleet where we were, to day—The sick & wounded being distributed among the fleet I cannot, not [note] their several conditions, those on board this (the Julia,) doing will—

3
Still lying at anchor waiting for a fair wind—or something else—The wounded doing well

4th
At Anchor, in York, harb^r waiting for the Storm to subside—

5th—
Still at Anchor, wind high.—min sickning—& miserably crowded in the hole of the Ship—

6th
Not weighed anchor yet wind, high, weather stormy & boisterous—

7th
Storm subsiding at night cold & chilly—min complaining much of Diarrheas & Dysenteries—the wounded doing far better than could be expected, in such a miserable condition—

8th—
Weigh'd Anchor, & got under way, for Niagara, arriv'd here at 5 ock. laned [landed] the Troops[29]—this morning one man died in the hole; merely, I believe, from sufocation as he had not been much ill except a slight wound on the back by a stone from the explosion,—had not time to examine him—

9th
Tents struck, at *Four-mile-Creek* four miles from the garrison.— Genl Boid,[30] takes com^d of the Brigade—

10th
The Fleet, sail'd for Sackett's Harbour, this morning, before Sunrise—carrying part of the sick & wounded, & are expected to bring on more Troops from the harbour,—

May 11th
This morning arriv'd from Oswego, in Sail-Boats, part of the 2^d Reg^t Artill^y, between three & four hundred.—[31]

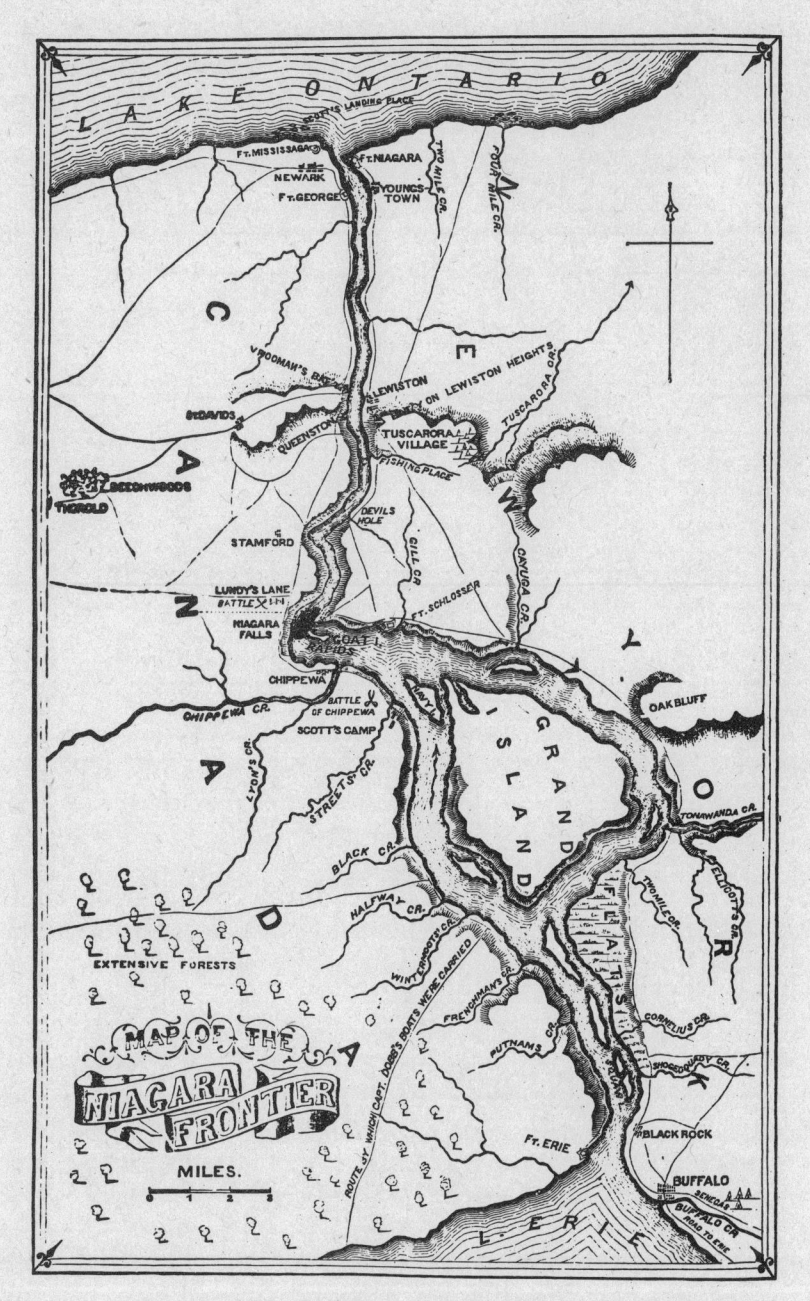

THE NIAGARA FRONTIER

QUEENSTON IN 1812.

Beaumont's General Notebook

In the after-noon I attended the Sale of *Genl Sheaffe's*[32] baggage, at public auction—taken at York—saw his most superb Scarlet coat sold for $55. which I presume cost not less than $300 it was the most elegant thing I ever saw, it was most elegantly embroydered in *Gold* and of the finest quality —his other things sold very high, being good & much wanted by our Officers—I purchased nothing—

12—13, 14, & 15th
Nothing worthy of note—hav'nt been out of Camp

16th & 17th
Nothing worthy of remark

18
Visited the *Falls of Niagara* that Great Natural Curiosity which at one view impresses the mind the mind of evry sensible beholder with sublime & reverential, Ideas—To contemplate the magnificent works of creation in viewing, such an immense colum of water, precipitated with such tremendious velocity, over a stupendious heighth, 200 feet perpendicular descent— raising from its force a mountain of foam, & clouds of fog, forming all the beautiful prismatic colours of the rain bow almost within your reach would force the incredulity of an Atheist, to acknowledge the existance of a God! In passing from the Garrison up the River had, a plain uninterupted view of *Fort George*, his Maesty's Garrison about a mile above Fort Niagara on the opposite side the mouth of Niagara River & of all the settlement on that shore, to the Falls—a distance of 18 miles, which are pleasant & handsomely situated— Queenstown, on the Brittish side & Lewistown, on our side the river are very pleasant, Villages Queenston, is situated at on a flatt, at the foot of a pretty high hill—on which is a Fort, where, Genl Van Ransellear,[33] was defeated & Genl Brock[34] killed—

Chipaway[35] is A Small Village one mile above the Falls, very pleasantly situated, on the banks of the Niagara River—

Beaumont's General Notebook

19th

Returned from the Falls visiting an Indian, Village about 3 miles off the road—was much delighted at some particular manoeuvers that occured—They appear to have been industrious, in cultivating their farms—Their farms were pleasant their land well tilled—

20th

Part of the Fleet returnd from Sackett's Harbour laden with troops, also about 400 from Oswego arrivd in boats—

21

The rest of the Fleet, excepting, the Ship, arriv'd to day, bringing, in the whole, about 1800. men 13 boat loads from Oswego also arrivd to day, with about 500. men

22—

General Orders for preparing for Battle, & an attack on Fort George—

23th, 24th, 25th, 26th—

Waiting for orders to embark—

27th Embarked at at break of day—Col Scott,[36] with 800 men for the advanced Guard—supported by the 1st Brigade comd by Genl Boyd—mov'd in concert with the Shipping, to the enemy's Shore & landed under the Enemy's Battery, & in front of their fire under cover of our shiping with surprising success, not lossing more than 30 men in the engagement tho the enemy's whole force was placed in the most advantageous situation possible—notwithstanding we routed them from their mounted & chosen spot, & drove them out of the country, took possession of the Town (Newark) & Garrison—Killed of the Brittish rising 100, wounded rising 200, prisoners 100—[37]

28th Part of the army proceeded to Queenston 6 miles above caus'd the Enemy to evacuate that Garrison, took some prisoners—

Beaumont's General Notebook

29th In peacible possession of the Fort—The Enemy retreating for Kingston.[38] *Com^d in the G Hospital*

30th no altiration the fleet sails for S Harbour

31st as usual, fair well in the place—

June 1st 1813 as we were—

2[d] Genl Winder's[39] Reg^t mov'd for—a part unknown to me

3[d] Fir'd a Feu-de-joy in consequence of Genl Geo Provost's defeat, in an attempt to land his troops at Sacketts Harbour & burn & destroy that place[40]

4th Nothing remarkable

5th " "

21 Mov'd the wounded from the Hospital, in the Garrison, at Newark to Lewiston on our side[41]—took a walk into the Country—return'd just before Tattoo, & retird to rest.—recommenced duty in Genl Hosp^l. Lewiston, 28th June—continued duty till 13th Aug. whin being unwell, & order'd to Ft. Geo. (suspended active duty

August 22[d] rec^d orders to repair to Fort George immediately—Going—

[*Several blank pages*]

[*Next page, upside down*] 3.00—Foresyths bill[42]
  50—for Boatman

[*Following page*]

TRAVELLING JOURNAL FROM PLATTSBURGH TO MACKINAC 1820

May 6th 3.A.M.—left Plattsburgh in the Steam Boat Congress & the *people* enjoying the refreshing influence of "Natures Sweet restorer, balmy sleep"[43]—(excepting a few, whose anxiety was too great)—passed very pleasantly on by Burlington V^t.

Beaumont's General Notebook

Essex, N. Y.—Saw Miss Deming & Miss French on the dock—but could not speak to them—passed up by Crown point—Ticondaroga—Northwest Bay—Basin Harbour—to White hall—stoped at Rocks—viewed the *big-ditch* & Locks[44]—took post coach for Albany

5. ok morning. Capt Ezra Smith—Misses Char^t Taylor—Mary Angus Peters & Fisk in compy—arrived at Sandyhill[45] at 10. ok A.M. Saw Rev. Mr Rogers—Uncle Dan[46] Josiah & Aunt & Clarissa—all will—took breakfast—attended forenoon Church— Dined (Mr Rogers with us) at *Beards*—took Post Coach at 1 ok & proceeded on down the North river, through several most delightful Towns—to Watertown[47]—Lansingburgh Troy, to Albany, where we arrived about 8.ok in the evening—the Ladies almost over come with fatigue—*Supped & retired*—

Miss Peters & Fisk, took Stage for Pittsfield, *Mas* at 3 ok. A.M. —Miss Taylor & Angus, took Steam Boat for New York at 9.A.M. I remained in Albany, till next morning at 3 ok & took Stage for Hartford Conn^{ct} & arrived there at 8.ok P.M. Stoped at *Morgan's Stage house*—proceed the next morn'^{g} to Lebanon, arrived at my Mothers at about 3 ok. P.M.—found them all well—& in good & easy circumstances—Staid 36 hours & took my mother & wint to New London—Saw Lucretia—Ann & Abel[48]—all well &c—Staid 18 hours & went on to South Kingston in Rhodisland—to See my Sister—found her well & happy, I believed—Staid 12 hours & returned—nothing of consequence has yet occured—*& finally* I dont believe them will worth taking the trouble to record before I get to Mackinac—so I will stop writing

Took passage in the Canal Boat, Western Engineer, from Whitesburgh, 4 miles from Utica & proceeded through the *big-ditch* to *Macedonia*[49] 7 miles from Auburn—A more useful & Stupendeous work could not have been *conceived, planned* & put *into execution* than this Canal[50]—To see navigable streams diverted from their natural course, & carried through the heart of an inland country for hundreds of miles, by means of man & upon which glide, in *easy, quick* & uninterrupted

State Prison at Auburn.

Cayuga Bridge.

Beaumont's General Notebook

course, boats of almost any burthen, upon a perfect plane, or level except now & then a Lock—astonishes a reflecting beholder & excites a solemn reverence—even for the ingenuity & perseverance of man—The Great Western Canal diverts the Navigation of the Western Lakes—& waters from its natural course down the St. Lawrence to Canada & from there to the ocean, & brings it through the midst of our Western States—into the North River to New York & then into the ocean—Nothing can be plasanter than to pass through the canal in the passage boats for you have nothing to disturb the most plasant feeling—being perfectly safe from every apprehension of danger of any kind—gliding smothily along upon the surface of still water at the rate of 5 miles an through a most delightful country—in plain view, & mostly through— young handsome flourishing villages—rich & well cultivated farms covered with a luxurent growth of cultivated vegitation —lofty forests—& will stocked with rich herds of cattle— Should the canal be completed upon the contemplated plan & carried through from Lake Erie to Albany—it will convert the *once* Western wilds into a cultivated garden—it will be like a living stream through the midst of a plain yard—May heaven avert *any* & *every* thing like political interuption—to so noble, grand, & useful an undertaking——

Arrived at Aúburn a very pleasant & flourishing Town—7 miles west of the Canal, at 3 ok P.M. on the 25th Inst—in this place a *States prison*[51] is building of Stone & Iron—with a very large yard which incloses about 3 Acres & the wall built of Solid Stone 12 or 15. feet high & 6 or 4 feet thick—there were about 200 convicts in the prison at this time I visited the prison in company with Mr White of Rome—went all over & examined it throughout could but admire the cleanliness, order & good condition of the prisoners & overseers—visited the United States Arsenal at Rome—found it in very neat order—visited Hamilton College[52]—Clinton a most delightful Site—in Auburn Saw an *elephant*, 14. ft high & every way in proportion—also—a *Ma-got*,[53] a *Leopard* & 2 monkeys—left Auburn at 4 ok. A.M. 26 in Stage for Buffalo—passed through

Cauga[54]—crossed the Lake over a bridge a mile long[55]—*Geneva*—a very pleasant & flourishing town—*Waterloo Avons*—*Canandagua*—Bloomfield—Genesee—Clarence—Batavia—& Williamsville—all very pleasant & flourishing towns to Buffalo 27th 6 AM — at Canandagua the Rev Dr Morse & son[56] came on board the Stage from whom I anticipate deriving much benefit & instruction as we shall probably proceed together to *Mackinac* he being on a mission among the Indians of the country—West & South west &c

Arrived at Buffalo on Saturday 27. Inst.—May remained at this place over Sunday—attended Church—heard young Mr Morse preach—or rather tried to hear him—saw Mrs Goodsell, formerly, D. Day took tea with her as an old acquaintance—

—Monday morning, 29th Started from Buffalo went to Black Rock[57]—2 Miles in company with Dr. J Morse & Son—crossed over to, Waterloo U. C. & procceded to the *Falls of Niagara*—through *Bartie*[58] *Chippewa*,—viewed the field of Battle[59]—passed on to Bridgewater & viewed the Battle ground at *Lundeys-lane*[60]—Dined at Wm Foresyth's[61]—viewed the *falls* above & below on Canada Side—crossed over & viewed below & above on the American Side—crossed back & proceeded to Queenston heights, viewed the Garrison—composed of a Sergeant's guard & 14 men—crossed the Ferry at Queenston over to Lewiston called on B. Cook Esqr & his Fathers family—Staid over night—in the morng came up on the American Side to the *falls*—viewed what is called Divil's-hole about half way between Lewiston & the falls—it consists of merely of a transverse fishure or excavation in the perpendicular limestone banks of the River about 150 feet high of no other extraordinary appearance than a hidious precipice with confused mass of Stones, dirt, & trees lying on the bottom—came to the falls & crossed over the famous Bridge built by Judge Porter[62] across the rapids just above the falls, extending onto Deer Island[63] in the middle of the river & just above the precipice—viewed the Island as thousands have before—Saw the perfect Rainbow about 9. ok in the morning—also saw it

THE PORT OF BUFFALO IN 1813.

PUT-IN-BAY.

the evening before on the opposite side—came from the falls to Black rock on the American Side—went on Board the Steam Boat Walk-in-the-Water[64] for Detroit. May 30—4.P.M.

31st Got under way at 9. ok this morning—fair wind & pleasant weather—go at the rate of 9 miles an hour—looking over an old newspaper, came across *Doct Franklins,* *"project for attaining moral perfection"*[65] to wit—"It was about this time I conceived the bold & arduous project of arriving at moral perfection; I wished to live without committing any fault at any time & to conquer all that either natural inclination or custom might lead me into—As I knew, or expicted I knew, what was right & wrong, I did not see why I might not always do the one & avoid the other. But I soon found I had undertaken a task of more difficulty than I had imagined; while my attention was taken up & care employed in guarding against one fault, I was often surprised by another habit which took the advantage of inattention: Inclination was sometimes too strong for reason. I concluded at last that the mere speculative conviction, that it was our interest to be completely virtuous, was not sufficient to prevent our slipping, & that the contrary habits must be broken & good ones acquired & established before we can have any dependence on a steady, uniform rectitude of conduct.—For this purpose therefore, I tried the following method

In the various enumerations of the moral virtues I had met with in my reading, I found the catalogue more or less numerous, as different authors included more or fewer ideas under the same name

Temperance, for example, was confined to eating & drinking; while by others, it was extended to mean the moderating every other pleasure; appetite, inclination, or passion, bodily or mental, even to our [avarice] & ambition—I proposed to myself, for the sake of clearance, to use rather more names, with fewer ideas annexed to each, than a few names with more Ideas; and I included under 13 names of virtues, all that, at that time occured to me as necessary or desirable; annexed to each a short precept, which fully expressed the extent I gave to its meaning

These names, of virtues, with their precepts, were,

1st *Temperance*—Eat not to dullness—drink not to elevation—
2d *Silence*—Speak not but what may benefit others or yourself—avoid trifling conversation—
3d *Order.*—Let all your things have their plane;—let each part of your business have its time—
4th *Resolution.*—Resolve to perform without fail what you resolve—
5th *Frugality.*—Make no expence but to do good to others, or to yourself;—i.e. waste nothing.—
6 *Industry*—lose no time be always employed in something useful; cut off all unnecessary actions
7th *Sincerity.*—Use no hurtful deceit:—think innocently & justly & if you speak, speak accordingly
8th *Justice.*—Wrong none by doing injuries, or omitting the benefits that are your duty.—
9 *Moderation*—Avoid extremes: forbear resenting injuries so much as you think they deserve—
10th *Cleanliness*—Tolerate no uncleanliness in body, clothes, or habitation
11th *Tranquility*—Be not disturbed at trifles, nor at accidents, common or unavoidable—
12th *Chastity.*—*Rarely use venery*, but for health or offspring: never to dulness or weakness, or the injury of your own or anothers peace or reputation—
13th *Humility.*—Imitate Jesus or Socrates—

My intention being to acquire the habitude of all these virtues, I judged it would be well not to distract my attention by attempting the whole at once; but to fix it on one of them at a time; & when I should be master of that then to proceed to another, & so on, till I should have gone through the whole 13; & as the previous acquisition of some, might facilitate the acquisition of certain others, I arranged them with that view as they stand above. *Temperance* first, as it tends to procure that coolness & clearness of head, which is so necessary where constant vigilance was to be kept up & a guard maintained against the unremitting attraction of ancient habits, & the force of perpetual temptation.—This being acquired & established, *Silence* would be more easy; & my desire being to gain knowledge, at the same time that I improved in virtue, & considering that in conversation it was rather obtained by the use of the ear than of the tongue, & therefore wishing to break the habit it was getting into of prattling punning & jesting (which only made me accessable to trifling company) I gave silence the second place.

This & the next in *order*, I expected would allow me more time to attend to my project & my studies.

Resolution once become habitual, would keep me firm in my endeavors to obtain all the subsequent virtues—*Frugality* & industry relieving me from my remaining debts & producing affluence & independence, would make more easy the practice of *Sincerity & Justice, &c—*

Conceiving that according to the advice of *Pithagoras* in the golden verses, daily examination would be necessary, I contrived the following method of conducting that examination—

I made a little book in which I alloted a page for each of the virtues—I ruled each page with red ink, so as to have seven colums to one for each day of the week, marking each colum with a letter for the day—

I crossed these colums with thirteen red lines, marking the beginning of each line with the first letter of one of the virtues, on which line, & in its proper colum I might mark, by a little black spot, every fault I found upon examination to have been committed respecting that virtue, upon that day—I determined to give a week's strict trial & attention to each of the virtues successively

Thus in the first week my greatest guard was to avoid even the least offense against *temperance*, leaving the other virtues to their ordinary chance, only marking every evening the fault of the day.—Thus, if in the first week, I could keep my

Beaumont's General Notebook

first line marked T, clear of spots I supposed the habit of that virtue so much strengthened, & its opposite so much weakened, that I might venture extending my attention to include the next; & the following week keep both lines free from spot —Proceeding thus to the last, I could get through a course complete in thirteen weeks & four courses in a year—

And like him who having a garden to weed, does not attempt to eradicate all the bad herbs at once which would exceed his reach & his strength, but works on one bed at a time & having accomplished the first, proceeds to the second: so I should have, I hoped, the encouraging pleasure of seeing on my pages the progress made in virtue by clearing, successively, my lines of their spots; till in the end of my numbered course, I should be happy in viewing a clean book after a 13 week daily examination"—

On the morning of the 31st May, left Black Rock[66] passed up by Fort Erie on Canada Side & Buffalo on the American—also the Towns of Erie, Grand river, Cleveland, Sanduskey & Put-in-Bay—near where the Naval Battle between the British & American fleets was fought in 1814 & victory gained by Com Perry[67]—passed by Malden[68]—(C. side) ascending the Detroit River—

—The Fort at Detroit is a regular work of an oblong figure, covering about an acre of ground—The parapets are about 20 ft in height, built of earth & soded, with 4 bastions, the whole surrounded with pallisadoes, a deep ditch & glacis—It stands immediately back of the Town[69] & has strength to withstand a regular siege, but does not command the river there are now   troops stationed there under the Com^d of—[70]

June 3^d Rode down to the *Spring* Wells & crossed over to *Sandwich*, (C.a) a small French village about 3 miles below Detroit —Fort Michilimackinac,[71] is handsomely situated on the S.E. side of the Island of this name on a buff Rock, rising from 1 to 200 feet from the water, almost perpendicular in many places, extending about half way round the island—It overlooks & of course commands the harbour, a beautiful semicircular basin of about one mile in extent, & from 1- to 5 or 6 fathoms in

Beaumont's General Notebook

depth, & sheltered from Lake Huron by two Islands stretching across its mouth, & leaving only a narrow channel by which to enter the harbor—there is a rise of ground in the rear of the Fort—on which is built a stockade, defended by 2 Block-houses & battery in front—There is a bomb-proof magazine in the fort

This Island (Mackinac) is Seven & a half miles in circumference— It is heighest in the center, handsomely crowning, resembling as you approach it at a distance, a turtles back which gave name to the Island—*Michilimackinac signifies a Turtle*—the ground on which the fort stands is 150- or 160 feet above the level of the Lake & 100 yards from the Shore—it is neatly built & exhibits a beautiful appearance from the water—on the N.E. Side—near the Shore & 80 feet above the Lake is an arched Rock—20 ft in diameter at top & 30 at the bottom or *base* Near the center of the island on a plain stands an insolated conical rock in the form of a sugar loaf 50 feet in height—which is perforated in various places, & the holes are filled with human bones—in an other part of the island is a rock called the *skull rock* which exhibits a similar appearance

June 3^d Reported to Genl A. Macomb[72]—rec^d his invitation to dine with him—accepted—Saw Mr Hatch, from Burlington Vt. formerly in the US. Qtr Ms Dep^t.—Introduced to the Rev Mr Montiethe,[73] Clergiman of this place—Introduced to Capt Cross formerly of the U. S. Arty—now an Atty of *Kaskaskias*,[74] *Illin^s. Teritory*—Visited the Cantonment found appearances rather indifferant—observed very strong symtoms of dissepation among the officers of the *Garrison* 3 June

4th Attended Presbyterian Church in the fore part of the day— heard a discourse from the Rev Dr Morse—Dined with Capt Hatch—attended the Catholic Church in the afternoon— witnessed the great anual ceremony of the celebration of our Saviour it was a great ceremony & *I think*, a great burlesque on religion—

Sunday 4

Beaumont's General Notebook

June

Monday 5—
Nothing worthy noting today—wrote a letter to the Surg[n] Gen[l].[75] for permission for private practice at Mackinac[76]—wrote what I *called a friendly letter* to Miss Charlotte Taylor[77]—Steam Boat left this for Black Rock—4 ok P.M.—gave Cap[t] Jo[s] Cross late of U.S.A. now a Lawyer of Illinis Ter—a letter of recom[n] to Mr Swetland[78] of *Plattsh*—Accidentally came acrosst a new *Poem* by *Samuel Woodworth*[79] Called—"The Poems—Odes, Songs, & other *Matricular effusions*—of *Samuel Woodworth*, Author of "The Champions of Freedom" &c"—S[p]ent the evening in perusing the work—it is a very interesting publication & highly worthy to be read in my humble opinion—& from which I extract the following lines as very applicable to my feeling, to wit,

"*Valedictory* or
the minstrel's farewell to his Lyre
Whin Fate's stern fiat dooms fond friends to part,
What thrilling pangs pirvade the feeling heart!
With ardent glow the proffer'd hand is press'd,
While the moist eye bespeaks the aching breast;
The final gaze, we, linger, still renew,
Dreading the last, the painful word—*Adieu*.

So I—a bird of passage—wont to rove—
Have oft been doom'd to leave the friends I love;
Have oft been fated to endure the smart
Which now afflicts my lacerated heart;
That heart, alive to every finer glow,
Enrapturing joy—or ecstacy of wo!"

Tuesday 6th *June*
Saw *Aunt Mary Hunt* as we used to call her whin she lived with Col. Snelling—I had not thought of her (not knowing she was there) untill she came out of a house & spoke to me as I was passing—She was a little embarrassed at the thought of being seen to hail me as I passed but only served to highten her *beauty*—She blushed like the *rose*—so crimson was her

Beaumont's General Notebook

youthful cheek, that it made even the *sun* look *pale*—She was very glad to see me, & hear from her friends in Pla^h after whom she made much inquiry, especially *Aunt Debby*[80] & Mr Green's family—I staid 30 minutes & left her still blushing

perused Alex Mackenzies travels[81] principally to day from which are made the following (to wit)

KNISTENEAUX INDIANS, NAMES OF THE MONTHS

May—Atheiky o Pishim—Frog moon
June—Oppinu o Pishim—The moon in which birds begin to lay
July—Aupascen o Pishim—D° when bds cst fths [birds cast feathers]
August—Aupahou o Pishim—D° young bds b^n fly
Sep^t.—Waskiscon o Pishim—D° when Moose Deer cast their horns
Oct^r.—Wisai o Pishim—The rutting moon
Nov^r.—Thithigon Pewai o Pishim—Hoar-frost moon
      Kuskatinayoui o Pishim—Ice moon
Dec^r.—Pawatchicananasis o Pishim—Whirlwind moon
Jan^y.—Kushapawasticanum o Pishim—Extreme cold moon
Feb^y.—Kichi Pishim—Big-moon—Old moon
March—Mickysue Pishim—Eagle moon
Ap^l.—Niscaw o Pishim—Goose moon

Wednesday, June 14th 1820

Nothing of consequence transpired for 10 or 12 days past—Spent my time principally in reading—writing some for Revd Dr Morse—drew off several maps—dined in the Canton^t 2 or 3 times—made few acquaintances & less *visits*

Started this morning at 4 ock in the Steam Boat Walk-in-the-Water for Fort Michilimackinac—had on board Gen. Macomb, Col Wool[82] Revd Dr Morse & many other gentlemen—had a fine breeze & fair weather—a thunder shower between 12 & 1 ok—Adop[t]ed the following maxim this day.

Trust not to man's honesty, whether Christian—Jew—or Gentile.—Deal with all as though they were rogues & villains, it will never injure an honest person & it will always protect

Beaumont's General Notebook

you from being cheated by friend or foe. Selfishness, or villany, or both combined, govern the world, with a very few exceptions—

at Sunset arrived at the lower end of Lake Huron—where the boat anchored for the night—here stands Fort Gratiot[83] a hansome little Fortification erected since the

[*following 4 lines at the top of succeeding page*]

> Oh—D—— my heart a vacuum feels,
> Your image only I can see;
> And wheresoever my body reels,
> My spirit wings its way to thee—

War—on a beautiful site—attended the *Insp^r Genl—Col Wool* on his inspection of the troops of this Post.—Saw Mrs *Julia* Hunt & returned on board the Boat—got under way at 3 ok next morning—& passed thr° Lake Huron—& arrived at Mackinac on the 16- of June 10 ok eve

17th Attended the Inspection of the Troops at this Garrison with Genl Macomb & Col J. E. Wool—Dined with Capt Pierce[84]—&c. &c. &c.

18th June. Assumed the charge of the Hospital & commenced Duty in U. S. Service—

19. to 27th Nothing extraordinary occured during this time—Obtained 2 horses of Capt Pierce—& procured a private waiter on the 26th Inst..—

!......! My thoughts are *nightly & every night, & all the nights* constantly with thee & faithful servants, are they, to the little divinity of Love—*Morpheus* sends them flying, fervent, faithful messengers of sleeping thoughts, to bear my love to you Oh, could I come & go as easily I would lay my glowing cheek, where, silently they rest upon thy swelling bosom & sweetly press those lips I love—On how long doth seem our separation, —anxious indeed am I to know our final prospects—were our present happy anticipations to be destroyed & our *hopeful, heart-sustaining prospects* cut off—oh how cheerless—difficult & desparate would be the future scenes of life—A deadly

VIEW OF MALDEN, WHERE THE BRITISH SHIPS WERE BUILT.

MAJOR GENERAL ALEXANDER MACOMB

Beaumont's General Notebook

banishment! A dark benighted world!—A hopeless—joyless life!—Could I not think of you by day & dream of you by night, there would be no zest in life—no stimulus to act—no wish to live. *You* are the soul of my existance—for you I live—I think—I act—& your dear image, do I cherish with increasing fervency & love—

June 18th Wrote to my friends—Dr Foot[85]—Dr S. B.[86] G. Freligh,—Dr B J Moores[87] my mother—& reported to the Surgn Genl & Gn Macb[88]—

July 17th To Dr S Beaumont & Dr Wm. Mason & Thos Green—went with the others 26th July

July 26th wrote to
John Beaumont[89]
Peter Thatcher
Dr S. Fuller[90]
Robt McPherson
I. C. Platt[91]
Dr L Foot & D——

Augt 18th wrote & forwarded to
I. W Anderson
Bates Cook
Charlotte Taylor
Mary Angus
Mrs I. C. Platt
Mr G. Freligh & Lady
Doct Foot on business
Sent $215- Dolls by D Stone

Sept 5. to Judge Delord[92]
Wm Swetland &

Augt 20 C Deming—

Elevated to a point, level with the Pale-faced moon viewing her silver visage in the watry mirror—I can contemplate &c—Daylight-dawn Aurora's harbinger

August 1st 1820

Made out my pay a/cs from May 1st—to July 31 complete, & forwarded them by Capt Pierce to be exchanged for a Draft

[63]

Beaumont's General Notebook

$250 to be sent on to Platts[h] for the payment of a Note of $200 with interest from Feb. 1820
[*Written diagonally across the above*] Capt Pierce brought these back *unpaid*—

Pay a/c. in Pocket Book made out to 31st July, 1820 & rec[d] of A. Phillips,[93] P.M. 3[d] Infy, Sept 1820

9th Sept 1820—Commenced a Diary of conduct on Dr Franklin's plan for attaining Moral perfection[94]

Reading *Shakespeare*, to day. I judged the following extract worth copying—

"Love all, trust a few, Do wrong to none: be able for thine Enemy, rather in power, than use; & keep thy friend under thy life's key: Be checked for silence, but never taxed for speech"—[95]

10 Rose at 6 ok, visited my pat[s] in village, & discharged Garrison duty before 9 ock A.M.—Settled my Hosp[l] a/cs with com[y]. & perused scriptures & Pope's Essay on man till eve—rec[d] letters from Platts'[h] & spent the evening in happy perusal & fanciful sociability—retired at 10 P.M. with only 2 little blots on my Book

11. Spent this day wholly in performing professional duties principally with Cap[t] Knapp   Vcc[d]. Col Boyd's[96] Infant—

12th Visited Cap[t] Knapp. Wrote letters & attended Court this day—

13
14 Merely performed the common avocations
15 of life & professional duties
16

---

17. to 24th nothing *remarkable*. Wrote to Dr Foot & De——g
    Dr S. B— Nancy Platt
    my sister Lucy—

---

to 30th Nothing remarkable came to pass this Mo.

MACKINACK, FROM ROUND ISLAND.[4]

RESIDENCE OF ISAAC C. PLATT IN PLATTSBURG, N. Y.
Used as British headquarters in War of 1812.

Beaumont's General Notebook

Oct 1st Wrote to Tommy Green by Mr Crooks,[97] remitting $50.. to Dr Morse, transmitting a specimen of Composition—pr Mr Crooks—Oct 4th reading Shakespeare, copied the following Maxims:

    I hate ingratitude more in a man, Than lying, vainniss, babbling drunkness, or any taint of vice, whose strong corruption inhabits our frail blood—Shkspeare—[98]

Oct 11 forwarded letters, dated 7th to Dr Foot & Dr.
                      Mrs I. C. Platt
Letters   Dr Morse with box &c
                      Br Abel Beaumont

Extrt *Autolicus* doleful ballads in Shakespeares plays[99]—How an usurer's wife was brought to bed with twenty money bags at a burden: and how she longed to eat adders heads & toads carbonado'd

---

Extt Cobbet—says Admiral Knight—Cochran & Hardy married American Ladies—that to go America without a wife & come back unmarried, argues that a man is not made of flesh & blood—

King Henry. "Fair Catharine! most fair; will you vouchsafe to teach a soldier terms, that will enter at a lady's ear, & plead his love-suit at her gentle heart." Shakespeare[100]

      The moon is up & in the surgy[?] *Mirror*, of the starry firmament, views her pale face & o'er this the dancing waves, expand her streams of light & sheds her paler rays on Mc nac's rocky
m   shores, to awake my thoughts & sighs of absent friends! a lovely eve by Heavens!—To sit & view the undulating surfaces of broad *Michigan & Huron*—like two reflective mirrors beautifying each the other—The sombre shade of night had meditation . . . .[101] to muse awhile on tender friendship—& happy scenes of seasons past—& then to dream of friends far off & pleasures yet to come—with joys like these who would not be a *voluntary exile*—a year or two—& then once more enjoy the bliss of social love & friendship—to mingle Soul with Soul—to reciprocate the tender feeling—to exchange the

[65]

m   mutual thought—to hear the vow of sympathy—to see the sparkling tear of gratitude & feel the sacred impulse of faithful love & friendship! Onc more, I say, who would not be an exile?—

Ext^d "Why should we shrink from what we cannot shun?
      Each has his pangs, but feeble sufferers groan
      With brain-born dreams of evils all their own"
                              Byron

m   Morpheus kindly envelops my faculties & shids the benign languor of Sleep over my drowsy senses—&c—

D^r *A man* of sterling talents & pure integrity is a blessing to any people or country—

Alas! I pause—where *am I?*—Whom have I left behind to sigh in pensive sadness in yonder distant village—to pine amidst the cruel persecutions of open hostile enemies & invidious foes?— O, wretched thought begone!

[*Written vertically across this page:*]
    Blanchard has Leave of ac^{se} untill further ... Nov 10- 1820

[*Written vertically across following page:*]
    Come! lovely Sleep stupefy my senses & ease my pain! Come gentle Morpheus creep slowly on envelop my wearied faculties & shed thy benign languor over my drowsy senses— O D——[102] I must bid you good night & retire to dream of you dreams of unsubstantial bliss—12 ock.—going-going-gone— to bed—*to sleep*—to dream. Oh! ... *D. D. where are you?* 4 ock. *morn*—awake ...

A man of great talents without integrity is a dangerous pest to society—

A man of true integrity, with moderate talents is a useful member of community—

A man with neither talents or integrity, is a nuisence & a calamity to any people

I woke real from *dreams* of bliss & pleasures all my own—you will call me weak for penning my sleeping visions—but Morpheus brought such pleasant visions last night & so delighted me that when I woke it did not seem a dream—the impression yet remains & so congenial is it with my most ardent wish & truly comportant with my strongest hope that even the orient orb of day in all her golden majesty does not demonstrate the sweet . . . nor can expel from my enchanted mind

Shades of night—Me thought Dr D. that you were wounded, sick & distressed—forsaken by your friends & pursued by your enemies & . . . unhappy inteligence reaching me at McNac I resolved to fly to your relief & started in the midst of storm tempest & danger to pass the boisterous lakes in open tossing broken canoe I toiled nights & days amid perils, pains & almost unsufforable fates—narrowly & frequently escaping watery graves, the only distress of which I felt in the prospects of death was that I could not come to your assistance— that I . . . loose you!—but lost to you with you too I suffer'd not only the pains of sickness & persecutions—but the pangs of grief for the bereavement of your friends from whom you fondly expected relief & to whom you looked for resolution & support—with . . . confidence & trust in myself—Here ends the *painful* part—and oh . . . & happy the transition from . . . surmount . . . difficulties of the menacing elements—arrived at a haven of safety, where I met two of our friends from P. rushing forward in the extacey of joy to announce to me the final & happy result of your "affair in court" & congratulating us on our prospects of mutual felicity—they told me you had been ill—distressed, & most cruelly persecuted—but that you had now triumphed over your enemies—had vanquished the whole host of *envy & malice*—& was now healthy—cheerful & as happy as the prospects of libels could make you—*my spirits vanished!*—soared upon the pinions of love, & with the rapidity of lightning—was exalted on the wings of the wind— was with you—mutually enjoying . . . *tender trembling & . . . affectionate embraces of Love* . . . ! Ah! & the scenes that ensued!—no pen can describe it! no tongue can tell it! no not words nothing but the most vivid imagination—under the same . . . impulse—afterwards can give even a fair representation of the . . . scene—Here the visionary reverie vanished—

Beaumont's General Notebook

I woke in the extacey of joy—&... it was a dream *but a dream* making such deep impressions upon my mind that it seems to me even at this hour like a reality & I verily hope it *may be*— the true harbinger of the happy event it so fancifully exhibits —*Heaven grant the pleasurable*,—but avert the perilous & painful parts in my dream

Letters   Nov 15th wrote & forwarded to Dr Sam & wife—Dr Foot & D——, Brothers John & Abel & Sister Lucretia—Miss C. Deming—& Surgn. Genl. last dated *Octr*. appertaining to Garden—[103]

---

letters   Nov 21st forwarded letters to I. C. Platt, G. Freligh & Ann Smith—[104]

[*Written vertically in right-hand margin:*]
See Mavor's Universal Histy. M. Anquetil. Trans from the French from page 150, vol 4th to 180

Reading—Mavor's acct [105] of the comt of the Christian Religion in the A.D. 30. & spread—flourished & became most popular under *Constantine*—son of *Constantius*—colleague & successor of *Galinius* the colleage & successor of *Diocletian*, the joint Emperor with *Maximian*—It seems to have been doubted in the earliest ages, even by *Constantine* & the wise men of his times whether Jesus Christ, was *God or Man—real or imaginary*—miraculously & supernaturally concieved by the Vir. My.— any thing more than an unusually good & honest man of that age—& these minds were nearlly divided with regard to the Trinity—The Sectaries took their names from the subject of controversies—the opinion of *Arius*, first discussed in the councils of *Constantine* & the divinity of Christ, was triumphantly established—

Constantine, died in the 74th year of his *age* & 34th of *reign*—was buried in *Constantinople* & believer in the Christian relign was succeeded by his 3 sons—*Constantine—Constantius & Constans* to [whom] were assigned the possession & government of all the Roman provinces—Constantine the oldest—killed in

Hist

337

Page 180 to 181

[68]

s General Notebook

```
                   younger—*Constans.*—
                 favored Christianity & sup-

              om his empire by Magnentius a
            inated in his flight—he opposed

          er & murderer of Constans, was
     ntiu
          er a weak prince than otherwise
          cousin as his colleage—
          sinated by Domitian—Sylvanus
          soldiers at the instigation of

          ostate a college of *Constantius*—
          "Fame, which exaggerates all
          of truth in her account of Rome"   Page
          his subjects—succeeded—*Con-*    193
          ne with an unanimity & tran-      4th
```
quility, before unknown in the Roman provinces— vol
killed in battle against the Persians—32 old—3-yr
reign as *emperor*—a *wise Emperor* great man & able
general

AD 363 to

Jovian succeeded *Julian* he was a Chistian—reigned 11
mos & died on his way to Constantinople—
Valentinian—succeeded *Jovian* took his brother *Valens*
for colleague died 55 old—reign'd 12—
Valens—succeeded *Valentinian*—was a most cruel &
merciless prince—reign'd 16 yrs & died in his 54th—in
him & in his reign the seeds & principles of the inquisi- 219
tion seem to have first existed

A.D. 378

Vol *Gratian* & Valentinian—sons of *Valentinian* & suc-
4 ceeded *Valens*—one 17 yrs old & the other only 4—
219 when they began to reign—under these Monarchs, com-
    menced the *Monks*—*Hermits* or *anchorits*—

[69]

Gratian—was wise, virtuous & faithful, but indolent & irrisolute—died in his 24th year, reigned 7—
Valentinian—was like his brother—lived only 20 yrs—reign'd 16—& was smothered to death—*Eugenius*—after *Valentianian*—then *Theodosius*—50—16—who at his death divided his empire between his two sons *Arcadius & Honorius*—the first of these lived 31 yrs & Reignd 13.—

242 *Rome*—taken & destroyed by *Alaric*—General of the Goths & Huns—agains Arcadia about AD. 409—
The *City of Carthage*, said to have been 50 or 100 yrs older than Rome—founded by *Queen Dido*—was surrounded by triple walls, flanked at intervals by towers—between the walls under arcades were stables sufficient for 300 Elephants & 4000 horses, & forage sufficient for them all, besides barracks for 20,000 foot soldiers—The city was built on 4 small hills & on the highest stood the citadel—containing 700,000 inhabitants—Its first government is supposed to have been Monarchical— Vol 4th Page 334-35

The Moguls, under the reign of Jenghis Khan, used to exercise their troops in winter, by frightening the wild beasts of the forests—The Emperor orders the hunters to trace out a circle several miles in circumference—the officers then arrange their troops around & commence a warlike movement towards the center, driving in all the wild beasts before them & when they get them near together & surrounded in small compass so as to see all the beasts—they strike up martial musick of all kinds & hunters & soldiers shout & cry in such a manner, as to terrify the animals into perfect submission—making them loose all their native ferocity even *lions & tigers* crouch & *Bears & wild boars*, become affrighted & confounded!—The great Khan, & his principal officers then advance with their swords Bows, & arrows &c to slay the beasts— Vol 5th 172 & 3

Vol 5th 172 & 3

The Island of *St Helena* half way between *America &* vol
Africa & opposite the *Cape* of *Good Hope*—at which the 6.
English Merch^t vessels usually stop on their passage 56
from E. India—is said to be a pleasant place, containing,
cultivated lands meadows & wood—together with a
spring which forms a rivulet—here nature appears always
vol smiling & always with the freshness of youth—The
6. inhabitants have a fair com complexion & remarkably
57- ruddy enjoying good health & attain to great age—the
climate is healthy—heat morderated by the East
St Helena winds—people temperate & sober—never in-
dulge in any irregularity except for a few days
during the stay of the E. India Company, whom to treat
politely as guests, they transgress their usual bound-
aries—

---

vol 6   The Indians in their dances resemble the negroes of
364.   Africa

Being assembled in numbers—more or less—from 10
to 100 or 10,00 they form a circle around one or two
individuals who stand in the center & beat the music,
which consists of a pair of parchment or dried sheep or
dear skin, drawn over a bow or hoop, upon which they
keep up a constant monotonous sound, by striking upon
this skin, with a sort of bat, similar to a base-drum stick
—Excited by this music, they begin to move their limbs,
first moderately & then with great and increasing
agility untill the whole are in the most violent motion—
capering round & through each other—whooping &
clapping the palm of the hands on their mouths at the
same time, interupting the most hidious—sharp &
piercing screaches—

Their dancing, on the first view, appears to be
merely stamping with the feet, accompanied with con-
tortions of the limbs & a hollow murmuring noise or
grumbling

The performers move in a circular direction—
stamping with perfect uniformity with their feet ex-

actly keeping time with their music—increasing untill their whole frames are in the most violent commotion—they then break, intermix with each other, utter the most horid shrieks—beat the ground with their feet—hang down their heads—continue a low murmur—& renew their exercise—Their motions are sometimes quick & sometimes slow, but exhibits a kind of disorder, which however is not destitute of method, as it is renewed with the most perfect imitation—men, women & children all join in the ceremony—They continue these gambols for half a day—appearing before every place in town where they think there is any whiskey—untill they get so tired & intoxicated that they can no longer perform—they then fall down under the fences & sheds &c, & sleep out the rest of the day in a state of brutal filthiness

The first mention made of the name *Beaumont* as I discover, is in the history of *Navarre*—soon after the reign of *Don John* Emperor of Arragon in about the year 1480 descended from the family of Gaston da Foix——   Vol 7 150

With *scenes of triumph & trophies* of *Glory*—Louis 14th King of France, commenced his victorious career—about 1680   283

—Frederick 2d King of prussia—indifferent to the myrtle of Venus, meriting the two-fold laurels of Mars & of Apollo   Vol 8th 355

Letters—forwarded, by express from Drummonds Island,[106] Jany. 20th 1821, to Mr G Freligh & wife

Do   Do by own express, Feby. 1st to Dr's S B, Foot & D——
Do   Do. my reports to Surgn Genl. & a letter of appln for furlow & Saml's appt

---

Feby. 1st 1821—Commenced reading *Rollins* History—[107]

Vol 1st—*Nimrod*, the first founder of the Assyrian Empire—*Ninus* his son—the builder & founder & finish of Ninevah—*Semiramis*, wife to one of the Chief of Ninus' Army—(1,700000 strong)—directed him (Ninus) how to attack the City of Bactria & by which means he took it—her husband afterwards killed himself & Ninus—married her—She commenced building Babylon—

The *subject* of Homer's Iliad was the anger of Achilles, so pernicious to the Greeks, when they besieged Ilion or Troy —The subject of his *Odyssey* the voyages & adventures of Ulysses, after the taking of the city—

JOURNAL FROM MACKINAC TO PLATTSBURGH, AUG^t 1821[108]

Extra Augt 9th—4 P.M.—Left M^{c}nac—fair wind—fine weather—
$2.25 pleasant passage—some agreeable passengers—1 buffoon— 1 quack—1 Excentricity

10th Strong head wind—progress slowly—several *sea-sick* —so myself—2 P.M. wind so strong the S.B had to put back 15. miles—wind subsiding—she came about again at 4 P.M. & made good headway all night—

11th Pleasant weather—wind in favor—progress—6 miles an hour—entered the mouth of R. St Clair, about 5 P.M.— passed Ft. Gratoit.—ran down about a mile—Boat stopped
.50 to take in wood—passengers—some of them landed—got underway at sunset, & ran down the river—nearly 40 miles,
psg. in 4 hours—to the flatts & lay by till daylight—passed the
to Bf British vessel—*Wellington* in the flatts—aground—entered
$31 Lake St Clair, about 6 a.m. had a very pleasant passage that beautiful small Lake, most delightfully bordered on either side, by fine cultivated farms,—neat & commodious houses.—arrived at the city of Detroit at 10 A.M. of the

12th—dined at Col Mac's.—rode 20 miles into the country with Capt Pierce, to view his land in Oakland County & re-
13 turned next morning—dined at Col Mac's. at 2 PM—came on board S.B. at 4.—ran down the river to Malden in 2 hours, 18. miles— $ .50

14th—6 A.M. at *Sandusky bay*
—at 2 P.M. at Cleveland—
—at 6 P.M. at Grand river—
15 —at 7 A.M. at Erie—weather delightfully pleasant & wind fair, arrived at B.k Rk. [Black Rock] at 7 P.M. 51

Beaumont's General Notebook

$3.
$4.50
5.50
hours only from Detroit—came to Buffalo entered name on Stage book for Albany—paid to Cdga
16th arrived at *Canandagua* 9 ock p.m.—entered for Utica 4 ok. morn^g. Stage fare

[*A number of blank pages follow. Beginning at the rear of the notebook, the following notations were made on the last two pages:*]

Due from WB
Register of Notes given

J. Palmer[109]—Decr. 23, 1819	$27..87
Benjⁿ Gilman[110]	57 —
Ph Wheelock	20 —
John Walworth[111]	57..35
J. G. Freligh	20..00
R Ransom	11..25
A Parsons	11..77
James Trowbridge	3. 37
Clinton Allen	10. 91
S. & L Williams	100. 00

Due from B & Wk[112]

to H. & Hull	$500
Penf^d & Stevⁿ	176

[*Inverted, at the bottom of the page:*]

I can no way express my feelings so appropriately as by borrowing the words of an infant post, with whose productions you are in the *weekly, if not daily*, habits pirusing—

Due from W. B & G S.[113]

M Myres	$65..27
Cost to RHW	21..29
D. Merit & Son	18..58
L Ransom	329..31
Phen Wheelock	50..00
C D Tyler	938..94
Penfold & S	1000..—

[74]

Notes—PART II

[1] John Wolcott, *To Chloe*. Wolcott (1738-1819) was an English poet and satirist who published under the pseudonym of Peter Pindar.

[2] Robert John Thornton, *The Philosophy of Medicine: or, Medical Extracts on the Nature of Health and Disease*. Fourth edition, London, 1799, Vol. II, pp. 218-219.

[3] This passage, reprinted in Thornton, *op. cit.*, is from John Milton, *Paradise Lost*, Book IV, 641-656.

[4] Thornton, *op. cit.*, pp. 220-221. The first 18 lines, with slight variations, are from John Armstrong, *The Art of Preserving Health*, Book IV, 284-299. Lines 19-37 are from Mark Akenside, *The Pleasures of Imagination* [First version], Book III, 568-574, 586-598, 550-558.

[5] Thornton, *op. cit.*, p. 233.

[6] *Ibid.*, p. 240.

[7] *Ibid.*, pp. 240-241.

[8] *Ibid.*, p. 282.

[9] *Ibid.*, p. 307.

[10] *Cf*. An Epistle from Dr. Thomas Sydenham to Dr. Wm. Cole, treating of the small pox and hysteric diseases. *The Works of Thomas Sydenham, M.D., on Acute and Chronic Diseases; with Their Histories and Modes of Cure*. With Notes ... by Benjamin Rush, M.D., Philadelphia, 1809, p. 304.

[11] Although little is known about him today, Dr. Benjamin Chandler (1772/3-1818) was one of the prominent practitioners of the region. *Cf.* Jesse S. Myer, *Life and Letters of Dr. William Beaumont*, St. Louis, 1912, pp. 18-20.

[12] War with England having been declared on June 18, 1812, an army was quickly organized and sent to the Canadian frontiers. Brigadier General Joseph Bloomfield had some 8,000 men under his command in the Plattsburg area.

[13] "The village of Plattsburgh, comprising 70 houses, is pleasantly situated on the high bank of the lake. It is a place of considerable trade; mostly in lumber, which is rafted over the lake, and down the Sorel and St. Lawrence to Quebec. The courts for the county are held here." James Mann, *Medical Sketches of the Campaigns of 1812, 13, 14.* Dedham, 1816, p. 170.

[14] About 4 miles from Plattsburg on the Saranac River.

[15] Commanded by Brigadier General Zebulon M. Pike, for whom Pike's Peak in Colorado is named.

[16] Malone.

[17] Gouverneur.

[18] *i.e.*, the county seat, where the law courts were held.

[19] "Sackett's Harbour was the only secure port for a navy on the lake; where Commodore [Isaac] Chauncey had hauled up the armed flotilla, during the cold season, waiting the breaking up of winter, to re-assume operations against the enemy. To this flotilla, was added a ship of twenty-eight guns, built entirely of green timber from the wilderness, within three months; and which was in preparation to sail, as soon as the obstructions formed by ice were removed. Sackett's Harbour was protected by two batteries, and two block-houses." Mann, *op. cit.*, pp. 56-57.

[20] According to Mann, p. 58, the entire force consisted of 1,600 men.

[21] Major General Henry Dearborn from Massachusetts who had been Secretary of War in Madison's cabinet was in command of the U. S. Army along the northern frontier.

[22] Gad Humphreys, John Walworth, and Peter Muhlenburg, all captains in the 6th regiment infantry. U. S. *American State Papers*, Class V, Military Affairs, Washington, 1832, Vol. I, pp. 398, 409, 410. Walworth was evidently from Plattsburg, as he is listed at the end of this notebook among Beaumont's creditors, see p. 74.

[23] Benjamin Forsyth, Major in the Rifle Regiment. *American State Papers, l.c.*, p. 408.

Notes — Part II

[24] Thirty miles away, where Lake Ontario flows into the St. Lawrence River. Rumors were circulating that the British had concentrated their troops at Kingston.

[25] Now Toronto.

[26] General Pike, a very able soldier, was among those killed.

[27] For a full account of the battle *cf.* General Henry Dearborn's letter to John Armstrong, Secretary of War, dated Apr. 28, 1813, from York. *American State Papers, l.c.,* pp. 443-444.

[28] *Cf.* Dearborn's letter of May 3, 1813: "There was an immense depot of naval and military stores. York was the principal depot for Niagara and Detroit; and, notwithstanding the immense amount which was destroyed by them, we found more than we could bring off. General Sheaffe's baggage and papers fell into my hands. These papers are a valuable acquisition: I have not had time for a full examination of them. A scalp was found in the executive and legislative chamber, suspended near the speaker's chair, in company with the mace and other emblems of royalty." *American State Papers, l.c.,* p. 444. According to the terms of capitulation of the defeated town, all private property was respected.

[29] From Dearborn's letter to Armstrong, Niagara Headquarters, May 13, 1813: "Commodore Chauncey, with the fleet and troops, arrived here on the evening of the 8th, and in the course of the night the troops were debarked in a very sickly and depressed state. A large proportion of the officers and men were sickly and debilitated . . . It was deemed expedient to give them time to recruit their health and spirits, and in the mean time for the fleet to return to Sackett's Harbor, and take on board one thousand additional troops; . . . This change in the proposed system of operations has been rendered necessary by a long series of the most unfortunate winds and weather that could have occurred at this season, and such as could not have been contemplated." *American State Papers, l.c.,* p. 444.

[30] Brigadier General John P. Boyd.

[31] Commanded by Colonel Winfield Scott. Dearborn wrote: "Colonel Scott reached this [sic] yesterday in boats from Oswego, with three hundred men. He was seven days wind bound in different places, and narrowly escaped the loss of his boats and men. I had expected him on the 3d. I had almost given him up for lost." *American State Papers, l.c.,* p. 444.

[32] Sir Roger H. Sheaffe, major-general, in command of the British forces at York. He afterwards defeated the Americans at Queenston.

[33] Major General Stephen Van Rensselaer, assigned by Gov. Tompkins to head all the militia from St. Regis to Buffalo, attacked Queenston on Oct. 13, 1812. He was not supported by Brig. Gen. Alexander Smyth, who commanded the regulars at Buffalo. In the battle an American force of 6,000 men had been defeated by 1,600 British, with a loss of 1,000 men, because there had been no cooperation between the generals and discipline among the troops. *Cf.* Julius W. Pratt, The War of 1812, in *History of the State of New York* (Ed. Alexander C. Flick), New York, 1934, Vol. V, pp. 231-232.

[34] Sir Isaac Brock, commander of the British forces.

[35] Chippewa.

[36] Colonel Winfield Scott who in 1841 became Commander in Chief of the U. S. Army.

[37] *Cf.* Dearborn's report to the Secretary of War, *American State Papers, l.c.,* pp. 444-445.

[38] Beaumont's statement is incorrect. The British forces actually retreated only some 40 miles to Burlington Heights (now Hamilton).

[39] Brigadier General William H. Winder. During this pursuit of the enemy Gen. Winder was captured.

[40] Dearborn and Chauncey had all their men at the western end of Lake Ontario and left Sackett's Harbour protected only by 400 regular troops and several hundred volunteers and militia under the command of Major General Jacob Brown of the militia. Sir George Prevost, governor general of Canada and British commander in chief, landed 800 men on May 28 with the support of the guns of the British fleet. Under the very able leadership of Brown, the British were repulsed. Pratt, The War of 1812, *l.c.,* pp. 233-234.

Notes — Part II

⁴¹ Mann reports that the sick and wounded were moved to Lewiston because of its healthful location on elevated, dry land. The first temporary encampments on wet ground had proved very unsatisfactory. Mann, *op. cit.*, p. 62.

⁴² This notation was probably made when Beaumont visited Niagara Falls in 1820, for he tells us later that he dined at Forsyth's and took a boat across the river. *Cf.* p. 54 *infra*.

⁴³ "Tir'd nature's sweet restorer, balmy sleep!" The first line of Edward Young's *Night Thoughts*.

⁴⁴ The Champlain Canal, connecting Lake Champlain with the Hudson River. It was not yet completed when Beaumont visited it. *Cf.* Noble E. Whitford, The Canal System and Its Influence, in *History of the State of New York* (ed. Alexander C. Flick), New York, 1934, Vol. V, pp. 409-442.

⁴⁵ "Sandy Hill, a small delightful village in New-York State, two miles north of Fort Edward, on a high hill, overlooking Hudson's river from the east." Jedidiah Morse, *The American Gazetteer*, 2nd edition, London, 1798.

⁴⁶ Probably Dan Beaumont, his uncle, who was born April 20, 1763, fought in the Revolutionary War, and was wounded at the battle of Princeton. *Cf.* Myer, *op. cit.*, pp. 6-7.

⁴⁷ Waterford.

⁴⁸ Beaumont's brother and sisters.

⁴⁹ Beaumont's mistake: Montezuma.

⁵⁰ The Erie Canal. Construction on the canal was begun on July 4, 1817 and by May, 1820, the time in which Beaumont is writing, the section from Utica to Montezuma had been completed, a journey of 96 miles. It was 40 feet wide at the water surface, 28 feet wide at the bottom, and 4 feet deep. In this section there were 9 locks, each 90 feet long and 15 feet wide, with one unbroken level of 67 miles. The passage took 36 hours, at a cost of $4.00. On October 26, 1825, the complete canal was finished, with continuous passage from New York to Buffalo. *Cf.* Whitford, The Canal System and Its Influence, *l.c.*, pp. 297-336; Jedidiah Morse, *A Report to the Secretary of War ... on Indian Affairs, Comprising a Narrative of a Tour Performed in the Summer* of 1820, New Haven, 1822, Appendix pp. 62-63.

⁵¹ Established in 1816. This prison developed a system of discipline, the so-called "Auburn system," which was later adopted by most penal institutions in the country. The prisoners were confined separately in small cells at night, but took their meals and worked in the shops with their fellow prisoners, without, however, being able to speak with one another at any time. This was in contrast with the "Pennsylvania system" under which solitary confinement the entire day was practised. For a very interesting description of this prison by a visitor in 1830 *cf.* John Fowler, *Journal of a Tour in the State of New York, in the Year* 1830, London, 1831, pp. 90-94.

⁵² Hamilton College in Clinton, N. Y., was founded in 1798 by Samuel Kirkland (1741-1808), a missionary among the Oneida Indians. It was named for Alexander Hamilton, the corner stone was laid by Baron von Steuben, and Thomas Jefferson presented the shade trees surrounding the building.

⁵³ Barbary ape.

⁵⁴ Cayuga.

⁵⁵ Fowler, *op. cit.*, p. 95: "a most barbarous structure, built upon piles, and conveying the idea, if not the reality, of great insecurity; as the planks, or logs, upon which you pass, uncovered with gravel, soil, or other material, are of all shapes and sizes, heedlessly laid across from side to side, without nails or any kind of fastening whatever. In many instances I observed them scarcely resting upon the supports on each side, and the waters of the lake every where visible below; of course, as they were acted upon by the weight and motion of the coach and horses, they were perpetually jolting up and down, so that it was a matter of astonishment to me how the animals could pass over at the rate they did, a good brisk trot, without getting their feet between them; the accompanying noise and clatter, too, was any thing but agreeable."

⁵⁶ The Reverend Jedidiah Morse (1761-1826) and his son Richard C. Morse. Dr. Morse was a Congregational clergyman who is better known as the "father of American geography," and also as father of Samuel F. B. Morse, the inventor of the telegraph and

Notes — Part II

a famous painter. His *Geography Made Easy*, published in 1784, was the first to appear in this country. It was followed by *The American Geography*, 1789, which went through numerous editions. In 1819, Morse was commissioned by the government to study conditions among the Indian nations. The results of this survey were published in *A Report to the Secretary of War of the United States, on Indian Affairs, Comprising a Narrative of a Tour Performed in the Summer of 1820* . . ., New Haven, 1822. In this *Report* we find the following very complimentary reference to Beaumont (p. 17): "In the feeble state of my health, I felt it to be a peculiar smile of Providence, to be favored, as we were, from Canandaigua to Mackinaw, and during our stay at the latter place with the company of Dr. Beaumont, Post Surgeon of the 3d Regiment of the U. S. Army, a gentleman of much skill in his profession, and of most amiable and kind dispositions. To him, by means of his medical prescriptions and attentions, I feel indebted, under Providence, for the degree of health, which enabled me to fulfil my duties to the Government, probably even for my life."

[57] At the entrance to the Niagara River. It was then three miles distant from Buffalo; now it is incorporated within the city limits.

[58] Bertie, a township on the Canadian side across from Black Rock.

[59] On July 5, 1814, the American forces under Major General Jacob Brown defeated the British under General Phineas Riall.

[60] On July 25, 1814, Major General Brown and General Winfield Scott fought an indecisive battle with the British under General Gordon Drummond. Brown was twice wounded. After the war Brown remained in the Army and was Commanding General from 1821 to 1828.

[61] "The Pavilion, kept by Mr. Forsyth, is a lofty eminence above the falls, on the Canada side, affording from its piazzas and roof a beautiful prospect of the surrounding scenery. It is a handsomely constructed building, and can accommodate from 100 to 150 guests." *Cf.* G. M. Davison, *The Fashionable Tour: A Guide to Travellers Visiting the Middle and Northern States*, Saratoga Springs, 1830, pp. 270-271.

[62] Peter Buell Porter (1773-1844), a member of Congress from 1809 to 1813, who fought with distinction on the Niagara frontier in the War of 1812. He served as Secretary of War under President John Quincy Adams in 1828-29. Coincidentally, he accompanied Beaumont on the steamboat to Detroit.

[63] Beaumont's error: Goat Island. "The sensation in crossing this bridge over the tremendous rapids beneath, is calculated to alarm the traveller for his safety, and hasten him in his excursion to the island." Davison, *op. cit.*, pp. 271 f.

[64] The first steamboat to sail upon the Great Lakes. It was built at Black Rock, near Buffalo, in 1818 and was totally wrecked during a gale in the offing at Buffalo, Nov. 1, 1821. For a detailed description of the boat *cf.* George B. Catlin, *The Story of Detroit*, published by the Detroit News, 1926, pp. 232-237.

[65] From Benjamin Franklin's *Autobiography*.

[66] According to Morse's *Report, l.c.*, p. 16, other passengers on the boat included the commissioners for settling the northern boundary of the U. S. from the St. Lawrence to the Lake of the Woods under the 6th and 7th articles of the Treaty of Ghent. They included Major General Peter B. Porter (*cf.* note 62 *supra*) and the Hon. Anthony Barclay.

[67] Oliver Hazard Perry (1785-1819) who on September 10, 1813, completely defeated the British fleet commanded by Captain Robert Heriot Barclay.

[68] At the mouth of the Detroit River on the present site of Amherstburg, Ontario.

[69] Samuel R. Brown, *The Western Gazetteer; or Emigrant's Directory*, Auburn, N. Y., 1817, pp. 166-168 thus describes Detroit at this time: "There are three streets, running parallel with the river; these are intersected by six cross streets, besides several lanes. The situation of the town is agreeable and romantic. The buildings are brick, stone, frame, and in some instances, hewn logs; but two thirds are frame; some very fine and painted; there are about three hundred buildings of all descriptions, exclusive of the suburbs, or 'Cotes,' extending above, as far

Notes — Part II

as lake St. Clair, and below, as far as the river Rouge, which appear to be a continuation of the town. The principal streets are wide, and most of the houses have picketed gardens in the rear. The inhabitants are more than half French; the balance consists of emigrants and adventurers from various parts of Europe and America ... Learning is at a low ebb; yet there is a large number of men of genius and education resident in the city."

[70] Omitted by Beaumont.

[71] This description of Ft. Mackinac, together with that of the fort at Detroit, was probably copied from a travel book while Beaumont was still on board the steamer, although I was not able to locate the source. It is obvious on the manuscript that the preceding June 3 notation was squeezed in later. After the description of Mackinac the journal continues with his activities while at Detroit.

[72] Major General Alexander Macomb (1782-1841) was in command of the 5th district with headquarters at Detroit. Beaumont had previously served under him at the battle of Plattsburg in September, 1814. After General Jacob Brown's death in 1828, Macomb became commanding general of the U. S. Army, a position which he held until his death in 1841.

[73] Rev. John Monteith, a graduate of Princeton, was one of the first Protestant ministers in Detroit. He was sent there in 1816 by the American Board of Commissioners for Foreign Missions. In 1817, together with the Roman Catholic priest of Detroit, he established the University of Michigan and was its first president. Thirteen chairs were created, of which Monteith held 7 and the Catholic priest 6! *Cf.* Silas Farmer, *The History of Detroit and Michigan*, Detroit, 1889, pp. 556-7, 728.

[74] Kaskaskia, located near the mouth of the Kaskaskia River on the Mississippi south of St. Louis, was one of the chief towns of Illinois at this time. Although Beaumont refers to Illinois Territory, it had become a state in 1818, two years before.

[75] Joseph Lovell. *Cf.* note 24, Part I.

[76] The permission was granted. *Cf.* Myer, *op. cit.*, p. 82 for excerpt from Lovell's reply.

[77] One of his companions in the stage coach to Albany, *cf.* p. 52 *supra*.

[78] William Swetland (died 1864) was one of the most outstanding lawyers in northern New York. *Cf.* Mrs. George Fuller Tuttle, *Three Centuries in Champlain Valley*, Plattsburgh, N. Y., 1909, p. 8.

[79] Samuel Woodworth (1784-1842), American poet, playwright and journalist, the only work of whom is still familiar today is the words to the song "The Old Oaken Bucket." The *Poems, Odes, Songs*, etc., was published in 1818.

[80] Deborah Green Platt, Beaumont's future wife. Her father, Israel Green, operated the leading hotel in Plattsburg.

[81] Alexander Mackenzie, *Voyages from Montreal on the River St. Laurence, through the Continent of North America, to the Frozen and Pacific Oceans: in the Years* 1789 *and* 1793 ... First American edition, New York, 1802, p. 73.

[82] Col. John Ellis Wool (1784-1869), who became a Brigadier General in 1841 and distinguished himself in the Mexican War. Dr. Morse wrote in his *Report*, p. 17, that Col. Wool "in his office of Inspector General, for which he seemed peculiarly well fitted, was on his route to visit and inspect the northern military posts." Other gentlemen on this trip included Capt. Ramsay Crooks and Mr. Robert Stewart, both of the American Fur Company, who were of particular interest to Dr. Morse because they had travelled to the Columbia River and knew a great deal about the Indians.

[83] Near the present site of the city of Port Huron. The fort was erected in May, 1814, and named for Capt. Charles Gratiot, U. S. Army, under whose supervision it was built.

[84] Benjamin K. Pierce, commanding officer at Ft. Mackinac, was the brother of President Franklin Pierce.

[85] Lyman Foote (1796-1846) from Wallingford, Conn., who like Beaumont was a career medical officer in the Army. A graduate in medicine of Yale College in 1816, he had lived for 8 years in the home of Prof. Benjamin Silliman who took a great interest in him. He married the daughter of Isaac C. Platt of Plattsburg (*cf.* note 91 *infra*). At the beginning of the Mexican War he was

Notes—Part II

appointed Medical Director of the army that invaded Chihuahua but died of fever and dysentery at Port Lavacca, Texas, before the campaign had begun. *Cf.* Nathaniel Goodwin, *The Foote Family: or the Descendants of Nathaniel Foote*, . . . Hartford, 1849, pp. 267, 331.

[86] Samuel Beaumont, William's cousin who is said to have studied medicine under him in 1815. When Beaumont left Plattsburg in 1820, Samuel took over his practice, and he later helped William to prepare the manuscript of the *Experiments and Observations on the Gastric Juice*.

[87] Benjamin J. Mooers (1787-1869), a nephew of Gen. Benjamin Mooers, one of the first settlers of northern New York. He began practising medicine in Plattsburg in 1810 and continued there until his death. *Cf.* William Richard Cutter, *Genealogical and Family History of Northern New York*, New York, 1910, Vol. I, p. 56. In 1818 Mooers had been Beaumont's patient, *cf.* Myer, p. 72, for facsimile of the case history.

[88] General Macomb.

[89] William's brother.

[90] This is probably Dr. Silas Fuller (1774-1847) of Lebanon, Conn., the home town of Beaumont. As a young man, he taught in the Lebanon school and at the same time studied medicine under a local physician. He began practising in 1798, was a surgeon in the War of 1812, and later became prominent in Connecticut medical and political affairs. He was probably Beaumont's teacher in the Lebanon school. *Cf.* Archibald Welch, A Biographical Sketch of Silas Fuller, M.D., *Boston Medical and Surgical Journal*, 1848, Vol. 38, pp. 109-115.

[91] Isaac C. Platt, son of Charles Platt, one of the first settlers of Plattsburg. During the War of 1812 the Platt homestead was used as the British headquarters and hospital. *Cf.* Tuttle, *op. cit.*, pp. 22-23.

[92] Judge Henry Delord (1764-1825), one of the foremost citizens of Plattsburg who entertained President Monroe when he visited the town in 1817. Born in Nîmes, France, he went as a young man to Martinique where he acquired a large plantation. The slave uprisings there forced him to leave the island and flee to this country where he settled in Peru, a small town in northern New York. For a number of years he had a general store and was postmaster of the village. In 1810 he moved to Plattsburg. When the British raided Plattsburg on July 31, 1813, his home was among those that were looted. Tuttle, *op. cit.*, pp. 89, 235, 239.

[93] Asher Phillips, paymaster, had gone to Ft. Mackinac in 1816. *Cf.* John Read Bailey, *Mackinac, Formerly Michilimackinac*, McMillan Edition, 5th revision, Ann Arbor, 1904, p. 200.

[94] *Cf.* pp. 55-58 *supra*.

[95] Shakespeare, *All's Well That Ends Well*, Act I, scene I.

[96] Probably George Boyd from Maryland, the Indian Agent at Mackinac. *Cf.* note 103 *infra*.

[97] Ramsay Crooks, general director of the American Fur Company in the settlement on Mackinac Island.

[98] Shakespeare, *Twelfth Night*, Act III, scene IV.

[99] *The Winter's Tale*, Act IV, scene III.

[100] *King Henry V*, Act V, scene II.

[101] Writing unintelligible. This and the next few pages are very faded and contain a number of indecipherable words, indicated by dots.

[102] Undoubtedly Deborah Green Platt, his future wife.

[103] Mr. George Boyd, the Indian Agent of the district, wanted a portion of the fort garden for the site of a new building. Beaumont's letter protested against this proposal and pointed out the harm which would result, since there was no other suitable place to cultivate fresh vegetables for the garrison and medicinal plants for the hospital. His rather strong letter is reprinted in Myer, pp. 89-91.

[104] Probably the sister of Beaumont's future wife who had married Col. Melanchton Smith, a prominent Plattsburg citizen and first editor of the Plattsburg *Republican*.

[105] Beaumont's reference is unclear. Although George F. Mavor did publish a *Universal History*, actually Beaumont's notes are taken from Louis Pierre Anquetil's *A Summary of Universal History*, translated from the French. Beaumont's page numbers

Notes — Part II

correspond to the edition Philadelphia, 1805-1809.

[106] Located on the strait connecting Lake Huron and Lake Superior. It contained a British garrison, and every June thousands of Indians within a circuit of five or six hundred miles came to the island to receive presents from the British government, as a reward for their services in the War of 1812. *Cf.* Morse, *Report*, p. 54.

[107] Charles Rollin, *The Ancient History of the Egyptians, Carthaginians, Assyrians, Babylonians, Medes & Persians, Macedonians, and Grecians*. This extremely popular history, first published in French in 1730-38, was translated into English and came out in a number of American editions in the first part of the 19th century.

[108] Beaumont does not give us any indication here of his reason for returning to Plattsburg. Actually he went back to be married to Deborah Green Platt, with whom he returned to Mackinac shortly afterwards.

[109] John Palmer came to Plattsburg in 1810 from Hoosick, N. Y. He was one of the first trustees of Plattsburg village when it was incorporated in 1815 and was appointed District Attorney in 1818. *Cf.* Tuttle, *op. cit.*, pp. 65, 174.

[110] Benjamin Gilman (1780-1853) from Gilmanton, N. H., was assistant principal of the Plattsburgh Academy when it opened in 1811. Tuttle, p. 136.

[111] A fellow officer in the War of 1812, *cf.* p. 44.

[112] Beaumont and Wheelock. In 1815 Beaumont and German Senter, surgeon of the 29th Inf. in the War of 1812, entered practice together and opened a store selling "drugs, medicins, groceries, Dye woods, etc." Senter, who was still on Army duty, left soon afterwards and Wheelock took his place in the store business. *Cf.* Myer, pp. 60-61.

[113] William Beaumont and German Senter, the first business partnership of Beaumont. *Cf.* preceding note.

Index

A

Advantages of a cultivated mind, 40
Akenside, Mark, *The Pleasures of Imagination*, 75
Albany, N. Y., 52 f., 74
Allen, Clinton, 74
Allen, Maria, 6
Ambition, Of, 41
American Fur Company, 79 f.
Amherstburg, Ont., 58, 73, 78
Anatomy, 22, 24
Anderson, I. W., 63
Anger, On, 41
Angus, Mary, 52, 63
Animal heat, 20
Anquetil, Louis Pierre, *A Summary of Universal History*, x, 68-72, 80
Armstrong, John, *The Art of Preserving Health*, 24, 35, 40, 75
Armstrong, John, Secretary of War, 76
Auburn, N. Y., 52 f.
Auburn Prison, 53, 77
Avon, N. Y., 54

B

Bailey, John Read, 80
Bangor, N. Y., 44
Barbary ape, 53
Barclay, Hon. Anthony, 78
Barclay, Robert Heriot, 78
Bartlett, James, 17
Basin Harbor, Vt., 52
Batavia, N. Y., 54
Beaumont, Abel, 52, 65, 68
Beaumont, Ann, 52
Beaumont, Dan, 52, 77
Beaumont, John, 63, 68, 80
Beaumont, Lucretia, 52, 68
Beaumont, Lucy, 64
Beaumont, Samuel, 63 f., 68, 72, 80
Beaumont, William; birth and early years, x f.; medical education, ix-xii, 43; prescription writing, 32 f.; license to practise medicine, xii; case histories, xiii, 6-9, 12-15, 17 f., 26-31; surgical operations, 16, 30 f., 46 f.; performs autopsies, 6, 8, 31; surgeon's mate in the War of 1812, ix-xiii, 10-18, 26, 43-51; battle of York, xiii, 16, 46 f.; battle of Plattsburg, xiii; private practice and business at Plattsburg, xiii f., 74; post surgeon at Mackinac, x, xiv, 29-31, 62-73; diaries, x; diary kept during the War of 1812, 43-51; journey in 1820 from Plattsburg to Mackinac, 51-62; diary kept at Mackinac, 62-73; journal kept in 1821 of trip from Mackinac to Plattsburg, 73 f.; *Experiments and Observations on the Gastric Juice and the Physiology of Digestion*, ix, 80.
Bertie, Ont., 54
Biliary concretions, 6
Black Rock, N. Y., 54 f., 58, 60, 73
Blanchard, 66
Blanton, W. B., 35
Bloomfield, N. Y., 54
Bloomfield, Gen. Joseph, 26, 35, 75
Boyd, George, 64, 80
Boyd, Brig. Gen. John P., 48, 76
Bradford, James H., 14, 34
Bridgewater, Ont., 54
Brock, Sir Isaac, 49, 76
Brown, Harvey E., 34
Brown, Major General Jacob, 76, 78 f.
Brown, John, system of medicine, xi, 21-24, 35
Brown, Samuel R., 78 f.
Buffalo, N. Y., 53 f., 58, 74, 76
Burlington, Vt., xi, 51, 59; general hospital at, 35
Burlington Heights, Ont., 76
Burns, Robert, *Reliques of*, x, 28 f., 35
Byron, Lord, 66

C

Canandaigua, N. Y., 54, 74
Canton, N. Y., 44
Cathartics, 20
Catholic Church, 59
Catlin, George B., 78
Cayuga, N. Y., 54
Champlain, N. Y., xi
Champlain Canal, 52, 77
Chandler, Dr. Benjamin, x n., xi f., 32, 36, 43, 75
Chauncey, Commodore Isaac, 75 f.
Chicago, University of, ix n.

[83]

Index

Chippewa, Ont., 49, 54
Clarence, N. Y., 54
Cleveland, Ohio, 58, 73
Clinton, N. Y., 53
Cole, Dr. Wm., 75
Congress, Steamboat, 51
Constable, N. Y., 44
Cook, Bates, 54, 63
Covet, 12 f.
Crockett, Walter Hill, 34
Cromek, R. H., 35
Crooks, Captain Ramsay, 65, 79 f.
Cross, Captain Joseph, 59 f.
Croup, 21
Crown Point, N. Y., 52
Cullen, William, xi, 24 f.
Cutter, William Richard, 80
Cynanche, 11
Cynanche stridula, 21

D

Daniel, John Moncure, 18, 34 f.
Davison, G. M., 78
Day, D., 54
Dearborn, Major General Henry, 34, 44, 75 f.
Delord, Judge Henry, 63, 80
Deming, Miss C., 52, 63, 68
Detroit, 58 f., 73 f., 78 f.
Detroit River, 58
Diarrhoea, 10, 12 f., 16, 48
Diseases, difference between general and local, 23 f.; acute epidemic, 25
Drummond, General Gordon, 78
Drummond's Island, 72, 81
Dysentery, 10-13, 16, 48

E

Earth, on whose lap a thousand nations tread, 19
Elephant, 53
Erie, Pa., 58, 73
Erie Canal, x, xiv, 52 f., 77
Essex, N. Y., 52
Experiments and Observations on the Gastric Juice and the Physiology of Digestion, ix, 80

F

Farmer, Silas, 79
Fevers, opinions of various authors concerning, 24 f.; symptoms of, 20; acute, 4; autumnal, 6; inflammatory, 8 f.; intermittent, 3 f., 10-13, 15 f.; spotted, 4 f.; typhoid, 12; typhus, 10-13, 16

Fisk, 52
Foote, Dr. Lyman, 63-65, 68, 72, 79 f.
Forsyth, Major Benjamin, 44, 75
Forsyth, Wm., 51, 54, 77 f.
Fort Erie, Ont., 58
Fort George, 49-51
Fort Gratiot, 62, 73
Fort Mackinac, see Mackinac Island
Fort Niagara, 49
Four mile creek, 48
Fowler, John, 77
Franklin, Benjamin, *Project for attaining moral perfection*, x, 55-58, 64, 78
Freligh, G., 63, 68, 72
Freligh, J. G., 74
French, Miss, 52
From nature's continent immensely wide, 19
Fuller, Dr. Silas, 63, 80
Fulton, Sgt., 14

G

Gastric fistula, ix
Gastric juice, ix, 35
Genesee, N. Y., 54
Geneva, N. Y., 54
Gilliland, Dr. Samuel, 13, 34
Gilman, Benjamin, 74, 81
Goat Island, 54, 78
God, wonders of, 18 f.
Goodsell, Mrs., 54
Goodwin, Nathaniel, 80
Gouverneur, N. Y., 44
Grand River, Ohio, 58, 73
Gratiot, Capt. Charles, 79
Great Western Canal, 53
Green, Israel, 61, 79
Green, Thomas, 63

H

Haller, Albrecht von, x-xii, 3, 34
Hamilton, Ont., 76
Hamilton College, Clinton, N. Y., 53, 77
Happy Pair, The, 38
Hartford, Conn., 52
Hatch, Mr., 59
Hippocrates, 20, 33
Hopkinton, N. Y., 44
Humors, 20
Humphreys, Capt. Gad, 44, 75
Hunt, Mrs. Julia, 62
Hunt, Aunt Mary, 60 f.
Huntre, Mrs. Polly, case of, 26-28
Huxham, John, xi, 20 f., 35
Hydrocephalus Internus, 8

Index

I
Illinois Territory, 59 f.
Imitation, 41
Indian, village, 50; names of the months, 61

J
Julia, Schooner, 16, 44, 48
Julian, John, 35

K
Kaskaskia, 59, 79
Kingston, Ont., 45, 51, 76
Kirkland, Samuel, 77
Knapp, Capt., 64

L
Lacolle, Quebec, 34
Lake Champlain, xi, 35
Lake Erie, 53
Lake Huron, 59, 62
Lake Ontario, x, xiii
Lansingburgh, N. Y., 52
Lebanon, Conn., x, 52, 80
Leopard, 53
Lewey, 14 f.
Lewiston, N. Y., 49, 51, 54, 77
Lovell, Surgeon General Joseph, xiv, 18, 35, 60, 63, 68, 72, 79
Luckhardt, Arno B., xv
Lundy's Lane, Ont., 54

M
Mackenzie, Alexander, 61
Mackinac Island, x, xiv, 52, 54, 58-62, 65, 73, 79 f.
McMullen, James, 15
Macomb, Major General Alexander, 59, 61-63, 79
McPherson, Robert, 63
Malden, *see* Amherstburg, Ont.
Malone, N. Y., 44
Mann, James, *Medical Sketches*, xii f., 34, 75, 77
Mason, Dr. William, 63
Mavor, George F., 68, 80
Medical department of the army, xiv
Merit, D., 74
Mexican War, 79 f.
Michigan, University of, 79
Michilmackinac, *see* Mackinac Island
Milton, John, *Paradise Lost*, 75
Minderer, R. M., 36
Modesty, 42 f.
Monkey, 53

Monteith, Rev. John, 59, 79
Montezuma, N. Y., 52
Mooers, Gen. Benjamin, 80
Mooers, Dr. Benjamin J., 63, 80
Morgan's Stage House, 52
Morse, Dr. Jedidiah, xiv, 54, 59, 61, 65, 77, 79; treated by Beaumont, 78
Morse, Richard C., 54, 77
Morse, Samuel F. B., xiv, 77 f.
Muhlenburg, Peter, 44, 75
Myer, Jesse S., *Life and Letters of Dr. William Beaumont*, x n., xv n., 36, 75, 79-81
Myres, M., 74

N
New London, Conn., 52
Newark, Ont., 17, 50 f.
Niagara, camp near, x, xiii, 16; Falls, 49, 54, 77; Devil's Hole, 54; River, 45, 49
North River, N. Y., 52 f.
Northwest Bay, 52

O
Opium, 22
Oswego, N. Y., 48, 50, 76
Oxygen, 20

P
Palmer, John, 74, 81
Parsons, A., 74
Penfold, 74
Perry, Oliver Hazard, 58, 78
Peter's Apology, 37 f.
Peters, Miss, 52
Phillips, Asher, 64, 80
Phthisis, 15
Physician, idea of the best, 20; young, 21; lesson to, 22; deportment of, 25
Pierce, Capt. Benjamin K., 29, 62-64, 73, 79
Pierce, Pres. Franklin, 35, 79
Pike, Brig. Gen. Zebulon M., 34, 75 f.
Pindar, Peter, *see* Wolcott, John
Pittsfield, Mass., 52
Platt, Charles, 80
Platt, Deborah Green, 61, 66-68, 79, 81
Platt, Isaac C., 63, 68, 79 f.
Platt, Mrs. I. C., 63, 65
Platt, Nancy, 64
Platt, Zephaniah, xiii
Plattsburg, N. Y., xii-xiv, 11, 15, 34 f., 43 f., 51, 60 f., 64, 75, 81; battle of, xiii, 79 f.; Academy, 81
Pleurisy, 5 f., 11-13, 21

[85]

Index

Pneumonia, 11-15, 20 f.
Poems, 18 f., 37-43, 60
Pope's *Essay on Man*, 64
Porter, Judge Peter Buell, 54, 78
Powell, Dr. Truman, 32, 36
Pratt, Julius W., 76
Prescriptions, 32 f.
Prison systems, 77
Provost, Sir George, 51, 76
Psalm 139, 18 f.
Put-in-Bay, 58

Q

Queenston, Ont., 49 f., 76
Queenston Heights, Ont., 54

R

Ransom, L., 74
Ransom, R., 74
Reward of Attention to the Laws of Animal Oeconomy, 42
Reynolds, Mr., 7
Rheumatism, 10 f.
Riall, General Phineas, 78
Rogers, Rev., 52
Rollin, Charles, *The Ancient History of the Egyptians, Carthaginians*, etc., 72 f., 81
Rome, N. Y., 53
Rush, Benjamin, 35

S

Sackett's Harbor, N. Y., x, 15, 43 f., 47 f., 50, 75; battle of, 51, 76
St. Albans, Vt., xi, 43
St. Clair River, 73
St. Martin, Alexis, ix f.
Salmon River, N. Y., 44
Sandusky, Ohio, 58; bay, 73
Sandwich, Ont., 58
Sandy Hill, N. Y., 52, 77
Saranac, camp, 11, 43; river, 75
Saunders, William, 6, 34
Schomberg, 35
Scott, Col. Winfield, 76, 78
Senter, German, 74, 81
Shakespeare, William, x; *All's Well That Ends Well*, 64; *King Henry V*, 65; *The Winter's Tale*, 65; *Twelfth Night*, 65
Shaw, Pvt., case of, 29 f.
Sheaffe, Sir Roger H., 49, 76
Sigerist, Henry E., xv
Silliman, Benjamin, 79
Skull, fracture of, 29-31
Smith, Ann, 68

Smith, Capt. Ezra, 52
Smith, Col. Melanchton, 80
Smyth, Brig. Gen. Alexander, 76
Snelling, Col., 60
Social affection, 38
South Kingston, R. I., 52
Spring Wells, 58
Steel, 20
Steven, 74
Stewart, Robert, 79
Stone, D., 63
Sweet is the breath of morn, 38 f.
Swetland, William, 60, 63, 79
Sydenham, Thomas, xi, 21, 25, 35, 43, 75
Sylvius de la Boe, 19, 35
Synocha, 8 f.

T

Taylor, Miss Charlotte, 52, 60, 63
Thacher, James, 36
Thatcher, Peter, 63
Thornton, Robert John, *The Philosophy of Medicine*, xi, 36, 39-42, 75
Ticonderoga, N. Y., 52
Tilton, James, xiii
Tompkins, Gov., 76
Tonics, 20
Toronto, *see* York
Townsend, Joseph, xi, 19, 33, 35 f.
Trent, Capt., 16
Trowbridge, James, 74
Troy, N. Y., 52
Tuttle, Mrs. George Fuller, 79
Tyler, C. D., 74

U

United States Arsenal, Rome, N. Y., 53
Utica, N. Y., 52, 74

V

Van Rensselaer, Major General Stephen, 49, 76
Van Swieten, Gerhard, xi, 20, 35
Virtue, the strength and beauty of the soul, 39 f.
Vomits, 20

W

W., Mary Maria, case of, 7 f.
Walk-in-the-Water, Steamboat, 55, 61, 78
Walworth, Capt. John, 44, 74 f., 81
War of 1812, xi-xiii, 75, 80 f.; hardships, xii, 11 f., 34, 46-48; prevailing diseases, xii, 10-15, 34; march from Plattsburg to Sackett's Harbor, 15, 43 f.; American

[86]

Index

naval force, 16, 44; expedition to York, 16, 44-48
Washington, George, 25
Washington University School of Medicine, St. Louis, ix, xiv f.
Waterford, N. Y., 52
Waterloo, N. Y., 54
Waterloo, Ont., 54
Watertown, N. Y., 44
Watts, Isaac, 35
Welch, Archibald, 80
Wellington, ship, 73
Western Engineer, canal boat, 52
Wheelock, Phen, 74, 81
White, Mr., 53
Whitehall, N. Y., 52
Whitesboro, N. Y., 52
Whitford, Noble E., 77
Williams, L., 74
Williams, S., 74
Williamsville, N. Y., 54
Winder, Brig. Gen. William H., 51, 76
Wolcott, John, *To Chloe*, 75
Wonders of God, The, 18 f.
Woodworth, Samuel, *Valedictory*, 60, 79
Wool, Col. John Ellis, 61 f., 79
Work is done, The, 19

Y

York, battle of, 16, 34, 45 f., 76; explosion of powder magazine, 16, 46 f.
Young, Edward, *Night Thoughts*, 19, 41, 77

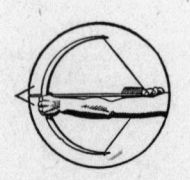

DESIGNED AND PRINTED BY
A. COLISH, NEW YORK